Making School
a Place
of Peace

CORWIN
PRESS

The Corwin Press logo—a raven striding across an open book—represents the happy union of courage and learning. We are a professional-level publisher of books and journals for K-12 educators, and we are committed to creating and providing resources that embody these qualities. Corwin's motto is "Success for All Learners."

Making School
a Place
of Peace

Theresa M. Bey
Gwendolyn Y. Turner

CORWIN PRESS, INC.
A Sage Publications Company
Thousand Oaks, California

For information address:

Corwin Press, Inc.
A Sage Publications Company
2455 Teller Road
Thousand Oaks, California 91320
E-mail: order@corwin.sagepub.com

SAGE Publications Ltd.
6 Bonhill Street
London EC2A 4PU
United Kingdom

SAGE Publications India Pvt. Ltd.
M-32 Market
Greater Kailash I
New Delhi 110 048 India

Printed in the United States of America

Library of Congress Cataloging-in-Publication Data

Bey, Theresa M.
    Making school a place of peace / Theresa M. Bey, Gwendolyn Y. Turner.
        c. cm.
    Inlcudes bibliographical references and index.
        ISBN 0-8039-6192-8 (c : alk. paper). — ISBN 0-8039-6193-6 (p : alk. paper)
        1. School violence—Prevention. 2. Peace—Study and teaching.
3. Activity programs in education. 4. School environment.
I. Turner, Gwendolyn Yvonne. II. Title.
LB3013.3.B49   1995
371.5—dc20   95-22884

This book is printed on acid-free paper.

96 97 98 99 10 9 8 7 6 5 4 3 2 1

Sage Production Editor: Diane S. Foster

Contents

Foreword   ix
     by *James P. Comer* and *Norris M. Haynes*

Preface   xi

About the Authors   xv

1. Moving Toward a Peaceable School   1
    Implementing Programs   2
    Reducing Violence   3
    Switching Over   4
    Changing Policies   5
    Setting Priorities   6
    Defining Peace   7
    Principles for Peace   8
    Planning for Peace   9
    Selecting a Change Approach   9
    Incentives for School Personnel   11
    Closing Thoughts   12

Let's Talk   12
Suggested Activities   14
Learning Exercises   14

2. Creating a Peaceable Environment   17
    The Principal's Leadership   18
    Creating a Safe School   19
    A Peaceable Environment   22
    Selling the School   23
    Making the Classroom Peaceable   25
    What Causes Conflict?   27
    Classroom Management and Discipline   28
    Closing Thoughts   30
    Let's Talk   30
    Suggested Activities   31
    Learning Exercises   31

3. Encouraging Peaceful Communication   35
    Forms of Communication   36
    Communication Among School Personnel   43
    Changing Negative Communication   44
    The Language of Peace   46
    Identifying Communication Styles   47
    Closing Thoughts   48
    Let's Talk   52
    Suggested Activities   52

4. Planning for Peace Across the Curriculum   55
    Revising the Curriculum   56
    The Hidden Curriculum   58
    Multicultural Peace   60
    Multicultural Curricular Approaches   62
    Multicultural Content   63
    Social Peace   64
    Planning for Change   65
    Closing Thoughts   66
    Let's Talk   67
    Suggested Activities   67

5. Changing Instruction: The Hard Realities   69

Differentiated Instruction 70
Multiple Intelligences 72
Understanding the Student 74
Conflicts 77
Problem-Solving Skills 78
Closing Thoughts 80
Let's Talk 80
Suggested Activities 81

6. Working With Parents 83
Parent-Child Communication 83
School and Family 85
Family Education 86
Parent Workshops 87
Adult Supervision 88
Instill Values 89
Parent-Friendly Support 91
Parent-Teacher Conferences 93
Closing Thoughts 95
Let's Talk 95
Suggested Activities 96

7. Building Family-School-Community Partnerships 101
School-Community Social Services 102
Family-Community-School Collaboration 103
Youth and Crime 104
Delinquency: What Are the Causes? 106
Denying Problems 108
Family-School-Community Action Plan 109
Closing Thoughts 115
Let's Talk 115
Suggested Activities 115

Appendix: Suggested Resources 117
Resource A: Social Peace Curriculum for Primary
and Elementary Schools 117
Resource B: Social Peace Curriculum for Middle
and High Schools 119
Resource C: Annotated List of Programs
and Curriculum Guides for Peaceful Schools 125

Resource D: Annotated List of Family, School,
    and Community Resources   131
Resource E: Resource Organizations for
    Teaching Peace   137
Resource F: Annotated List of Children's Literature
    for a Social Peace Curriculum   140
Resource G: Bibliography of Children's Books   145
Resource H: Professional Literature Related to
    Discipline and Classroom Management   150

References   153

Index   159

Foreword

For too many of our children, violence is a constant source of terror and fear. Many schools that once were safe havens from the violence that plagued homes and communities are now themselves experiencing significant increases in violent episodes. This is a major cause for concern, given the threat to the physical, psychosocial, and academic well-being of children that community and school violence poses.

Children are not born violent. Aggression and other antisocial behaviors are learned responses to conditions and circumstances in one's socializing environments: home, community, and school. The contextual forces that shape what and how children think and feel about themselves, and others, have much to do with the violence children experience and/or perpetrate in our communities and schools. Thus the experiences that we as adults provide for children, in schools and classrooms, in the media, in our homes, and our communities have a significant impact on their psychosocial and emotional health.

The school is a major socializing and character-developing agent in children's lives. Next to the home, and in some cases, in lieu of the home, the school has the most significant long-term influence on children's development. The school and classroom context, academic and extra-curricular activities, and the social development programs that we provide all help to shape and build character, protect children, and prepare them to constructively contributing members of society. Our approach to child development must, therefore, be a systemic ecological approach that underscores the total development of children. We must pay much closer attention to school climate issues and construct school environments that encourage, nurture, and support positive values and behaviors, by respecting and responding to individual and group differences as well as similarities.

This book sensitizes and informs us, not only about the need to make "school a place of peace," but also discusses strategies for doing so. It is a book that should be read by everyone who is concerned about reducing the risk of violence in our schools and increasing the chances for peace and the opportunities for success in school and in life.

James P. Comer
Norris M. Haynes
Yale Child Study Center
New Haven, CT

Preface

Is America's education agenda to reduce school violence creating more opportunities for children to live and learn peacefully?

In looking for answers to this provocative question, we found that no school, whether urban, suburban, or rural, is immune from societal ills. Today, children and youth encounter acts of harm, hostility, and frustration as a part of life. Some of them manage to cope with these difficulties, yet lack the skills needed to protect their social well-being.

As educators and concerned citizens, we must insist that our students learn conflict resolution, social problem-solving, and peacemaking skills. We also must teach them to behave in socially acceptable ways, to question and challenge injustices, to establish personal and academic goals, to understand their own rights and responsibilities, and to assume their future roles as the peacemakers of our society.

As the incidents of violence, retribution, and intimidation continue, so does the necessity for schools to infuse peace throughout all aspects of the educational process. Proactive peace planning is essential to prevent future hostilities, to reduce harmful conflicts, and to help children succeed academically. We can start this journey by promoting peaceful strategies and actions in our schools, homes, and communities. Peace is not just the absence of conflict or violence, but the practice of social harmony, cooperation, tolerance, and mutual respect.

This book is written for educators at all levels and individuals concerned about making school a safe, orderly place for students to learn and teachers and staff members to work. It will serve as a resource for persons interested in addressing the growing problems of violence among young people. Our primary intent is for readers to use it as a source of suggestive and commonsense guidelines to promote and increase peace.

The introductory content in Chapter 1 endorses the national commitment to have violence-free, peaceful, and productive schools. It includes an interpretation of peace and presents the principles for a peaceable school. In Chapter 2, ideas are suggested for a safe school environment and a crisis management plan. Next, Chapter 3 discusses various forms of communication for peaceful interactions among students, faculty, and staff members.

Content in Chapter 4 emphasizes the need for social and multicultural peace objectives in curricula designed for all subjects and grade levels. Chapter 5 advocates the use of differentiated instructional approaches and the development of multiple intelligences. In terms of practical ways for school personnel to work effectively with parents, Chapter 6 contains useful suggestions.

Collaborative support systems among local organizations, agencies, and services to create family-school-community partnerships are explained in Chapter 7, in addition to strategies for a peace -building action plan. Last, the appendix contains helpful resources divided into various categories: social peace curriculum, programs and curriculum guides, family-school-community resources, resource organizations, theme-based literature, children's books, and professional literature.

The concluding questions for each chapter, called "Let's Talk," provide opportunities for readers to discuss ideas and share information. The "Suggested Activities" at the end of each chapter are intended for course assignments, study groups, or professional development sessions; they will need tailoring to fit individual situations. Also, both Chapters 1 and 2 have activities designed specifically for classroom teachers to use with students. Although users of the book will differ, we would like to hear your concerns regarding biases or omissions. So, write (in care of Corwin Press) to tell us what pleases, puzzles, or perturbs you.

A vision for the book emerged as we worked on school-oriented concepts of peace with the American Educational Research Association Special Interest Group (SIG) on Peace Education. We would like to thank the members of the SIG for their commitment to peaceful schools and a nonviolent world.

Of course, a project of this nature could not have been completed without the support of family, friends, and our hard-working editors—Alice Foster, Diane S. Foster, and Marilyn Power Scott. We would like to thank all of you and the organizations who willingly provided us with information on request.

As leader author, Theresa owes a special debt of appreciation to Staff Development Director Wanda West, school principals, members of the Social Services Unit, and campus police in Bibb County Schools (Macon, GA) for sharing their professional knowledge. Gratitude is also extended to staff developers and school personnel in Atlanta City Schools and DeKalb County Schools.

Others who influenced this project include students and professional friends at The University of Georgia—foremost, the College of Education Dean, Russell Yeany. Further acknowledgment is extended to colleagues for their time in extemporaneous conversations: Carl Glickman, John Dayton, Duncan Waite, Mary Atwater, and Melvin Bowie. Also, the graphic artwork of Christine Miller at the University of Georgia Center for Educational Technology, the word-processing talent of Valerie Kilpatrick, and the typing services of Karen Orr contributed to this book.

Gwen wishes to thank the children in the St. Louis City and County schools for their insight, efforts, and dreams for a better world.

Theresa M. Bey
Gwendolyn Y. Turner

About the Authors

Theresa M. Bey, Ph.D., recognized for her work and publications in the area of mentor education, teacher education, and supervision, is a faculty associate in the College of Education, Program for School Improvement at The University of Georgia. Receiving a Senior Fulbright Scholar appointment in 1995, she served as lecturer and researcher for the Cyprus Ministry of Education and the Turkish Office of Education. As an active educator committed to school improvement and teacher development, she has presented her work in Brazil, China, Europe, Hong Kong, and Israel. Previously, she held a College of Education faculty position at East Texas State University and served as university coordinator for the Dallas Teacher Education Center. Being a former classroom teacher, a school-home-community relations administrator, and a teacher of undergraduate and graduate courses (e.g., curriculum, instruction, high-risk learners, urban education, supervision, staff development, group development), Dr. Bey consults nationally with schools and state departments of education. Currently, serving on national boards and committees her professional involvement continues, as well as work on her next book, *Mentoring for Teacher Growth and Development.*

Gwendolyn Y. Turner, Associate Professor of Education at the University of Missouri-St. Louis, has worked with students and teachers in urban settings, suburban neighborhoods, and rural communities to improve learning, promote literacy, and enrich learning environments. As a member of the St. Louis Professional Development Schools Collaborate, she works with classroom teachers to improve instruction, conduct classroom-based action research, enhance student motivation, and promote life-long learning. For the past 6 years, she has worked with academic and social enrichment programs for urban high school students. She continues to work with urban parents through family literacy programs that promote families working together to reach their dreams and aspirations. She is a member of the Association of Teacher Educator's Commission on School Violence Prevention. Her research and writings have focused on preparing teachers for urban settings, motivating reluctant learners, megacognition, and infusing peace education into teacher education programs. She has served as a consultant to schools in several states and has presented her work in several countries, most recently in South Africa.

PRINCIPLE 1

The school's commitment and vision should include the cultivation of peace throughout all aspects of the educational process.

❧ 1 ❧

Moving Toward
a Peaceable School

A commitment to make school a place of peace is one of the ultimate challenges in education. It's not too late for us to help children unlearn aggressive and disruptive behaviors. Despite being called the "lost generation," our children and youth are not lost but terribly misguided by impractical values. As aggressors, victims, or witnesses, they experience interpersonal violence firsthand, and they no longer feel safe from senseless fights or other dangerous incidents.

The national call to stop destructive behavior is widespread, as business and professional entities urge schools and communities to take action. One commission report states the following:

> Our [schools and communities] can intervene effectively in the lives of children and youth to reduce or prevent their involvement in violence. Violence involving youth is not random, uncontrollable or inevitable. Many factors, both individual and social, contribute to an individual's propensity to use violence, and many of these factors are within our power

to change. (American Psychological Association [APA] Commission on Violence and Youth, 1993, p. 14)

How often do you listen to neighbors, friends, or family members talk about violence? Your colleagues at school may mention fights on the playground, horrible news articles, incidents of neglect and abuse, or worse, attending the funeral of an individual who was a crime victim. These events make safety and security serious and unavoidable issues. Moreover, they could cause you to ask,

What can I do to make school a peaceable place for children?

Implementing Programs

One in every four students, regardless of their school level or achievement, feels that violence has lessened the quality of education in their school" (Metropolitan Life, 1993, p.7). The erosion of quality is a national concern, and students have noticed a difference—enough for educators to raise the following questions about programs:

- What kinds of programs are needed for hostile students to change their antisocial behavior and improve academically?
- What kinds of programs are effective in teaching misbehaved students the importance of social values such as caring, empathy, and respect?

As schools implement violence prevention programs, their primary focus must be a commitment to teach social values. Typically, the main focus of programs is a viable way to combat misbehavior. Research shows that middle and high school programs have not explicitly emphasized values, but they have emphasized the teaching of social skills as a way to promote peace (Cueto, Bosworth, & Sailes, 1993). Although these programs underscore social skills, there is another viable alternative: It is the integration of peaceable concepts, skills, and practices throughout the educational process as a way to combat violence.

Reducing Violence

Schools are supposed to represent a democratic society with a mission to educate, not to police children. (Tennessee Education Association and Appalachia Educational Laboratory [TEA-AEL], 1993, p. 5)

The mission to educate children has not changed, but what has changed dramatically is the mission against violence. School districts need security coverage to maintain violence-free buildings. Some of them have installed surveillance and warning devices to monitor students and check for weapons. Other forms of equipment used include ID badges, metal detectors, closed-circuit television, and walkie-talkies.

School boards concerned about increasing protection for students are appropriating funds for security expenses. A great deal of emphasis is placed on safety as school officials expect principals, teachers, and staff to follow strict disciplinary codes. Because they are legally responsible for student violence, school personnel must know how to intervene, gather evidence, and take action to remove a disruptive student from school.

If sudden acts of violence are stopped immediately, the level of student and teacher fear is manageable. This may not be the case when fights occur randomly. No one can feel completely at ease because such incidents are unpredictable. Weapons used by individuals in physical attacks, aside from guns and knives, might be scissors, pencils, rulers, or belts. Worried about being hurt, students generally feel less safe at school than teachers do, according to findings from the Metropolitan Life Survey (1993).

Children have become the victims and the witnesses of emotional, verbal, and physical violence (see Table 1.1). These acts fit within the definition of violence as "behaviors in which individuals intentionally threaten, attempt, or inflict physical harm on others" (National Research Council, 1993, p. 2).

Such behaviors make it extremely difficult for individuals not to be afraid in school. Put yourself in their place, think about your own uneasiness, how you fear different forms of violence, and the crimes that occur every day.

Table 1.1. Different Forms of Violence

Revolutionary Violence	Destructive Violence	Physical Violence	Verbal Violence	Emotional Violence
Massacre	Fighting	Bullying	Arguing	Agitating
Riot	Mugging	Grabbing	Cursing	Angering
War	Murdering	Hitting	Insulting	Blaming
	Poisoning	Kicking	Labeling	Condemning
	Raping	Pinching	Lying	Embarassing
	Shooting	Punching	Name calling	Ridiculing
	Stabbing	Pushing	Taunting	Scolding
	Stealing	Scratching	Teasing	Scorning
	Vandalizing	Slapping	Threatening	Tormenting

What can I do to prevent or reduce the chance of children being harmed by violence at school and at home?

Switching Over

What will the switch from violence to peace entail? At the onset, it entails a strong commitment from school personnel to work continually at the task of turning unruly behavior into calm behavior. Everyone in the building has to commit to helping students learn how to resolve conflicts and problems rather than fight. In addition, school employee involvement in school-home-community initiatives is important. Several initiatives to consider have been suggested by the Commission on Violence and Youth (APA, 1993). They include the following:

- Early childhood interventions directed toward parents, child care providers, and health care providers to help build the critical foundation of attitudes, knowledge, and behavior related to aggression
- School-based interventions to help schools provide a safe environment and effective programs to prevent violence
- Heightened awareness of cultural diversity and involvement of community members in planning, implementing, and evaluating intervention efforts

- Development of the mass media's potential to be part of the solution to violence, not just a contributor to the problem
- Limiting access to firearms by children and youth and teaching them how to prevent firearm violence
- Reduction of youth involvement with alcohol and drugs, known to be contributing factors to violence by youth and to family violence directed at youth
- Psychological health services for young perpetrators, victims, and witnesses of violence to avert the trajectory toward later involvement in more serious violence
- Education programs to reduce prejudice and hostility—two factors that lead to hate crimes and violence against social groups
- Efforts to strengthen the ability of police and community leaders to prevent mob violence by early and appropriate intervention

The implementation of these initiatives requires persistence and patience from everyone involved. No one should expect to transform schools or modify the behavior of disruptive students overnight. Transformation is a developmental process, so it is important to be realistic and plan for change.

Changing Policies

How might new or revised school policies strengthen the commitment to peace?

School policies enacted to alter behaviors and solutions to problems may not please everyone. The reactions of administrators and teachers are evident when they accept or reject traditional solutions. This point is eloquently addressed by Sarason (1993):

> The [stakeholders] of educational policy may adopt, proclaim, and take steps to implement a policy, but if that policy is not explicitly and directly geared to alter what goes on in the dynamics of life in the classroom—especially in regard

to alteration in power relationships—the policy is an exercise either in futility or irrelevance, or both. (p. 166)

Whether you agree or disagree with the relevance of educational policies, there is little time to debate the conditions of peace. Proactive policies to support peaceful teaching and learning are needed. In fact, they should go beyond the classroom to advocate change in home and community life.

An endorsement of school-community partnerships will lighten the heavy burden on teachers as "lone captains" in the effort to teach prosocial behavior. A policy for peace should consist of guidelines for school employees, parents, and students to learn the processes and skills of peacemaking.

If the guidelines propose a community-based commitment, then school-community planning and involvement will add new responsibilities to the already busy schedules of faculty and staff. They will need extra release time and professional development. School personnel must be prepared for their role in creating the peaceable school. In addition, school officials must be willing to seek additional support and resources from the state education department, school board, state legislature, and community.

Setting Priorities

The identification of school and community issues is important to local policymakers and program planners, enabling them to set priorities for peace based on an awareness of the community's history, pupil population, and funding sources. Equally important, they should identify future needs and consider changes that will affect (a) staff development, (b) curriculum, (c) assessment and placement of students, (d) counseling, (e) staffing, and (f) school-community relations (Leake, 1993).

In setting priorities for peace, remember, it is critical to emphasize what's best to help students concentrate on learning—not on violence. If necessary, expectations can be altered to better meet their needs. Listen to what the students have to say and the thoughts that make you question your actions.

Whose school is this, anyway?
Is it the students', the principal's, the teachers', and the parents'
equally?

A school, of course, belongs to the people. Therefore, decisions related to violence prevention should include faculty, parents, and students. They need an opportunity to assume ownership in identifying problems and finding solutions to antisocial behavior. A participatory school governance structure includes all three groups in decision making and uses consensus building as part of the problem-solving process (Duttweiler & Hord, 1987).

Consensus building might not be practical in a school where priorities and decisions are regulated by chief administrators. The governance structure is controlled and decision making happens as a traditional top-down, autocratic process in which solutions to problems are dictated. The authority exerted by school leaders can encourage or discourage the involvement of others in setting priorities to create a peaceable school.

Defining Peace

In planning for a peaceable school, the principal, faculty, and students will need to develop a definition for the word *peace* that is acceptable to everyone and matches the school's intent to infuse peace throughout the educational process. If no one definition can be developed to meet all expectations, then a general interpretation can be used. For example, "Peace is to prevent violence and to promote the qualities of social harmony, cooperation, and justice."

In the educational literature, peace and *peace education* are sometimes narrowly defined in relation to war, nuclear issues, and disarmament. In a broader context, peace education relates to "teaching about justice, about violence in all its forms, about survival and our future" (McConaghy, 1986, p. 249).

So far, peace "remains hidden in the educational literature, rather than actually practiced in the classroom" (Stomfay-Stitz, 1994, pp. 6-7). Having to compose a modern, school-related definition for the purpose of this book, the authors agreed to define peace as "behavior that encourages harmony in the way people talk, listen, and interact

Table 1.2 Specific Principles for a Peaceable School

School commitment to nonviolence includes the infusion of peace throughout all aspects of the educational process.

The classroom environment is a safe, orderly, and peaceful setting that contributes to positive thinking and learning.

Inclusive communication is the peaceful exchange of information and the sharing of feelings, decisions, and ideas.

A social curriculum serves the students' need to learn social responsibility and peacemaking skills.

Innovative instruction teaches students to consider the consequences of negative behavior and to solve conflicts peacefully.

Parent participation is encouraged to support children's learning of prosocial activities at home.

Collaborative partnerships and family-school-community networks implement programs to increase peace.

---

with each other, and discourages actions to hurt, harm, or destroy each other."

This definition complements prosocial behavior and nonviolent conduct. It facilitates the goal to create an inviting school where individuals interact, communicate, and behave in a positive manner (Purkey & Novak, 1984). Both the definition and the goal are intended for explicit use in education, but they can be adapted to suit other professions and institutions.

Principles for Peace

The seven principles recommended to guide the development of a comprehensive program for peace are discussed separately in each chapter throughout the book. They refer to peace in the following areas: (a) school commitment, (b) classroom environment, (c) communication, (d) curriculum, (e) instruction, (f) parent involvement, and (g) family-school-community partnerships (see Table 1.2). Individuals can adapt and apply the principles to reform teaching and learning by increasing practices to promote peace.

Table 1.3 The Seven Phases of Planning a Peaceable School

Phase	Activity	Question
1	Develop a Focus	What is a peaceable school?
2	Specify Needs	What are the concerns?
3	Reaffirm Commitment	Why should we take action?
4	Identify Principles	What do we want?
5	Design a Model	How do we get there?
6	Select an Approach	What strategies do we use?
7	Implement Plan	Are we ready to start?

Planning for Peace

Systematic planning for peace includes two key elements: collective involvement and shared decision making. These participatory elements can be guided according to the diagram provided in Table 1.3. It suggests seven phases of planning with accompanying questions inherent in making decisions.

In this progressive scheme, Phase 1 begins with the development of a focus, the goal to create a peaceable school. Data and information collected in Phase 2 provide an understanding of student and school personnel needs. Then, the needs, curriculum objectives, and educational requirements are meshed in Phase 3 to reaffirm the school's commitment to having a caring, safe environment. A further clarification of the commitment occurs in Phase 4—the identification of principles.

A peaceable school model is designed in Phase 5. It should describe and show links between school employees, parents, and other concerned citizens. The process of selecting an approach and preparing strategies to supplement the model is completed in Phase 6. Finally, in Phase 7 the plan to infuse peace into the educational process should be ready for implementation.

Selecting a Change Approach

Reforming the educational program to integrate peace is a step-by-step process. Once the school model (Phase 5) is completed, a change approach is identified, by choosing strategies to implement the model. Ideas for different approaches can be generated from the ones described shortly. These approaches represent various fields of study and make assumptions about schools and people who work to achieve reform (Deal & Peterson, 1991).

Human Resource Approach. Rooted in psychology, this change strategy targets the skills and needs of educators. It assumes that educators work best when their needs are met and they have the professional competence to do what is expected and needed of them. For example, individuals interested in topics related to the prevention of school violence can organize study groups or write "how-to" articles.

Structural Approach. Rooted in sociology, this strategy targets the formal structure and operation of schools. It assumes that schools operate best when goals are clear, daily activities have concrete objectives, employee roles are well defined, and individual efforts are linked to productivity, performance, and evaluation. For example, teachers coordinate efforts to use specific activities to elicit high levels of student achievement and low levels of misbehavior.

Political Approach. Rooted in political science, this strategy targets the political power and relations between constituents in the community. It assumes that additional school resources can be supplied by the influence and power of groups. For example, faculty and staff members invite powerful community groups and local businesses to sponsor child safety activities (e.g., health and safety fairs, nonviolent-book and media fairs, stop teenage smoking campaigns).

Free Market Economic Approach. Rooted in economics, this strategy targets financial benefit and competition for student enrollment. It assumes that educators will work harder if vouchers and school choice exist. For example, school personnel may use the cost of local taxes, educational funding, or violence prevention to recruit new students.

School Culture or Ethos Approach. Rooted in anthropology, this strategy emphasizes human conduct, values, beliefs, and norms in the behavioral patterns of people. It assumes that teachers and students are strongly influenced by the morale, mores, routines, and opinions about how things are done in their school. For example, school personnel and students may work cooperatively to establish a peace art center, a student court system, or a peaceable code of conduct.

Table 1.4 Incentives for School Personnel

Use the following statements to discuss and review incentives for faculty and staff at your school.
1. The professional accomplishments of school personnel are announced and published regularly in the news media.
2. An employee of the week is chosen for special recognition (e.g., academic excellence, changing student behavior, mentoring, etc.).
3. Teacher appreciation and recognition days are continual events.
4. Support systems and new resources are provided for school personnel.
5. Faculty and staff are encouraged to participate in professional activities (e.g., national and state conferences).
6. Administrative advisory teams and committees include school personnel, parents, and community residents.
7. Teachers are viewed and treated as professionals by students, staff, parents, and administrators.
8. Faculty and staff have adequate time and space to plan, work, and share ideas with colleagues.
9. Information about teaching innovations, changes, and continuing educational opportunities is made available to all employees.
10. Faculty and staff are praised and respected by district-level and building-level administrators.

A well-constructed change approach needs to include multiple strategies to ensure that everyone has a role in making the entire school a safe, calm place. Students should know how they fit within the "big picture" of the school as a whole. Preferably, the strategies will motivate individuals to exchange information and learn from others.

Incentives for School Personnel

Incentives to stimulate faculty and staff peace-building efforts include certificates, bonuses, or special privileges. Also, positive publicity renews employee pride, confidence, and energy. Recognition gives adults a sense of purpose, similar to what students may experience when recognized for their work. The statements shown in Table 1.4 can help in thinking about low-budget or in-kind incentives for personnel.

New resources and professional growth opportunities heighten the motivation of faculty and staff. Such incentives may magnify self-development and improve performance, yet do little to eliminate work-related frustration. In any position, school employees will encounter a certain amount of stress associated with the challenges of working with children, particularly disobedient children.

The tension attributed to student misconduct can dampen the enthusiasm of individuals who enjoy teaching. Admittedly, education is becoming an inherently stressful profession; employees (especially teachers) need to know how to deal with the psychological demands and the pressures of their work (Gold & Roth, 1993). A "day away" lunch hour outside the school campus or redeemable time-out coupons for the principal to cover a teacher's class for short periods may help to relieve stress.

In situations where teacher morale is low, incentives to promote employee satisfaction may not be enough, especially if the pressure is unbearable and faculty members want to transfer, resign, or request long-term sick leave. Anyone who suffers from emotional or physical discomfort cannot be highly productive or effective in the classroom. Administrators should think about employees' stress when scheduling or rescheduling meetings, because inconvenience is frustrating. Overall, acknowledgment of success and incentives encourages everyone to support peace for a change.

Closing Thoughts

This chapter invites you to give serious thought to planning for peace. Ask yourself, "Am I ready to move forward?" If so, gather general information about current school policies, programs, and activities using the "Getting Started" questions (see Table 1.5). Be willing to organize or serve on a committee to examine anti-social behavior, violence prevention, and school safety.

Throughout the phases of planning, suggest that committees include a cross section of school employees, parents, and local citizens. They can help conduct a survey to identify problems and possible solutions. Such activities are the first steps in moving toward a peaceable school.

Let's Talk

1. What is your definition of a peaceable school?
2. What type of school policy would you suggest to promote peace?

Table 1.5 Getting Started

The following questions are intended for use in gathering general information to start planning for peace; they are not a prescriptive checklist.

1. Does your school have a written policy to endorse peace, tolerance, or social harmony?
2. Do school policies explain how efforts to promote nonviolence should be maintained?
3. Does intervention help the troublemakers change their antisocial behavior?
4. Does your school recommend that teachers use a standardized approach to enforce classroom rules?
5. Does the school mission statement or strategic plan include an objective to improve student social problem-solving skills?
6. Is the local community informed about the school's disciplinary codes or the "zero tolerance" approach against violence?
7. Do students serve on school governance committees?
8. Are teachers willing to spend their personal time helping students before or after school?
9. Does your school provide mentors for new teachers and new students?
10. Does your school provide opportunities for the professional development of school personnel?
11. Does your school recognize or honor role models of peace in the local community?
12. Does your school emphasize the need for community residents to advocate and practice peace?
13. Do teachers promote student competition and cooperation in curricular and extracurricular activities?
14. How do school personnel and students display their school pride?
15. How do you help to create a sense of "family" or "belonging" at your school?
16. Does your school district conduct workshops on peer mediation or conflict resolution, or both, for faculty and students?
17. How does the school publicize positive events, activities, and accomplishments?
18. How many individuals in your school foster positive social interactions?
19. How many people are involved in making your school a place of peace?
20. Do you think the faculty and staff at your school will want to infuse peace throughout all aspects of the educational process?

3. Do you think school violence prevention is enough to modify antisocial student behavior?

4. How do you feel about security protection programs to guard students and adults at school?

5. What are some of the reasons teachers and students might not feel safe in school?

6. How might schools prepare students to think more about peace and less about violence?

7. In your opinion, what type of actions can schools and communities take to implement principles for peace?

Suggested Activities

1. Arrange for a school law resource person (e.g., school board attorney, school law professor) to meet and talk with school personnel, parents, and students about the legal responsibilities involved in efforts to reduce school violence. Take thorough notes or videotape the meeting for future use with new faculty and staff.

2. Rewrite the school philosophy or mission statement to include information about peace. Share a draft copy with colleagues for their opinions, then prepare a final copy to be considered for inclusion in the school handbook.

3. Gather a small group of your colleagues together to discuss and recommend changes to bring about positive social values.

4. Read the different forms of violence shown in Table 1.1, then prepare a list of ideas and activities to reduce antisocial behavior.

5. Refer to the seven phases of planning for a peaceable school shown in Table 1.3, then construct a "to-do list" to show the activities that would need to be completed for each phase.

6. Prepare a list of incentives for administrators to consider in recognizing dedicated school employees.

Learning Exercises

The following exercises can help introduce peacemakers and the concept of peace to students.

1. Have students prepare a list identifying persons they believe to be peacemakers. Once the list is completed, have them add their own names to the list. Then, ask students to tell why each person on the list is considered a peacemaker.

2. Have students respond to the following list of questions. Then, have them use the questions to interview someone who is not a member of the class. They can use a cassette tape player to record the interview and play it back in class.

   a. What is peace?

    b. What do you know about peace?

    c. What would you like to know about peace?

    d. Who are peacemakers?

    e. How are peacemakers chosen for their work?

    f. How are peacemakers recognized for their achievements?

3. Have students write responses to this open-ended statement: "I support peace because . . . "

After students complete their responses, ask them to share what they have written with the class.

4. Organize students into small groups and give them a choice in answering these "how does peace" questions.

    a. How does peace give you a sense of well-being?

    b. How does peace protect your future?

    c. How does peace help you appreciate diversity?

    d. How does peace get you to respect yourself?

    e. How does peace help you understand one another?

    f. How does peace change your attitude?

PRINCIPLE 2

The classroom environment should be a pleasant and peaceful setting, contributing to effective teaching, thinking, and learning.

❧ 2 ❧

Creating a Peaceable Environment

Our mission is to provide a safe, secure, and peaceful teaching and learning environment for all students and staff by protecting life and property.
San Diego City Schools (1995)

The greeting, "Welcome to Our School" is posted for everyone to see when entering the school, but if changed, it could read:

――――――

Welcome. Our school is a safe and peaceful place in which to learn.

――――――

Hospitable greetings display cordiality and convey a message about the school. In environments where harmony among people is the norm, a positive climate may exist for students to learn in calm, comfortable, and secure surroundings.

Likewise, teachers may plan interesting lessons, treat students equally, and maintain a well-managed classroom. The students think the rules are fair, the teachers like the students, and the content is meaningful. The school administrators emphasize academic development, minimize student disruption, and require regular attendance. These are only a few of the conditions needed for a peaceable environment.

Among the many factors necessary for a safe, inviting school, the three most important are (a) goals, (b) rules and procedures, and (c) staff-student relationships (U.S. Department of Education, 1993, p. 9). They support efforts to build a peaceable environment when

1. there is a strong emphasis on the school's academic mission;
2. there are clear discipline standards that are enforced firmly, fairly, and consistently; and
3. there is an ethic of caring that guides interpersonal relationships.

Such factors contribute to a trouble-free climate in which teachers and students can achieve educational objectives. They offer an opportunity for everyone to participate in making the school an organized, relatively quiet, and pleasant place.

The Principal's Leadership

An active school leader motivates and sets the tone for a purposeful school climate—one that generates the creativity and participation of teachers in sharing their uniqueness with others. Such a leader is supportive, accessible, open to ideas, and nonjudgmental in listening to the concerns of faculty, staff, and students. He or she simultaneously attends to school affairs, models peaceful behavior, and expects to be held accountable for successes and failures.

As a part of making everyone feel accepted, the principal learns the names of students and faculty and displays a sense of humor. Other leadership characteristics include the administrator's visibility and willingness to talk to students and faculty about school improvement. If the principal is a member of the school's instructional team, he or she should endorse teacher creativity and activities to transform the building into a hospitable place. For example, a decorative directory in the main entrance could display the names and room numbers of faculty, the school motto, and a picture of the mascot. Lively plants, photos, artwork, and banners throughout the school would also create a friendly as well as professional atmosphere.

When a principal is not the supportive instructional leader but a stern disciplinarian who maintains social order through punishment, teachers and students view leadership as control. They may receive little administrative assistance because the principal either is too busy or prefers to spend time on matters of school governance.

Chronic troublemakers consume the time of everyone, and they make it difficult to have a safe environment. In extreme situations, district officials have to respond and help the principal understand that chronic "problems with violence are not indicative of poor leadership" (Kadel & Follman, 1993, p. 21). An effective school leader welcomes the services of security personnel trained to deal with serious misbehavior and safety management.

Creating a Safe School

As concerns about safety increase, schools may have funded or nonfunded protection systems. A nonfunded, site-based safety system might function with the use of volunteer monitors, parent safety teams, or student hall patrols; a funded system might include a contract for services with the local police department or the hiring of peace officers as school employees.

One example of an extensive 24-hour protection system is the San Diego City Schools Police Services Department (1995). Serving a large urban school district with 196 schools, the department's staff consists of 34 sworn armed officers and 13 nonsworn community service officers. The protection services include response to a districtwide computerized fire and intrusion alarm system.

Before safety services are implemented, faculty, staff, and parents should be invited to offer suggestions on ways for officers to interact with students. When assigned to a school, peace officers can enforce school codes and teach students about violence prevention. In most cases, they will patrol the building, stop intruders, and question anyone loitering outside the building. They may also assist at athletic and school-sponsored events to prevent violence and supervise the movement of people.

Posting signs is another form of school security. They can direct visitors to sign in and out at the main office and wear an identification badge while in the building. In addition, signs remind students to be mindful of policies regarding weapons possession, drugs, locker searches, and rules about leaving campus. Parents should receive information about policies and be invited to make suggestions regarding

Table 2.1 Safe School Inventory

Directions: Check "Yes" or "No" for each item.

Yes	No	
___	___	1. Are unused stairwells and unused sections of the school closed off?
___	___	2. Are student lockers installed in areas where they are easily visible?
___	___	3. Are convex mirrors used to minimize blind spots and allow school monitors to see around corners?
___	___	4. Is playground equipment located where it is easily observed?
___	___	5. Is access to the roof limited by keeping dumpsters away from the building?
___	___	6. Are trees and shrubs trimmed to limit outside hiding places for people or weapons?
___	___	7. Are school grounds kept free of gravel or loose rock surfaces?
___	___	8. Is there vehicle access around the building(s) for night surveillance and emergency vehicles?
___	___	9. Do parking lots have speed bumps to discourage through traffic?
___	___	10. Is there a separate parking lot for students and staff who arrive early or stay late?
___	___	11. Are gates and fences secured with heavy-duty padlocks?
___	___	12. Is there a complete list of staff members who have keys to the building(s)?
___	___	13. Is graffiti removed from school property as soon as it is discovered?

SOURCE: Adapted from Kadel and Follman (1993).

school safety. A school-home-community group that meets regularly to discuss problems and security ideas is also helpful.

A secure environment conforms to the protective strategies listed on the "safe school inventory" (Table 2.1) and supplies both students and teachers with personal safety information. In addition, they are told to avoid wearing expensive clothing and valuable jewelry if thefts occur often. Sometimes student uniforms will solve the problem, reduce peer pressure, build school pride, and make it easy to identify students.

As for gang members, male and female, school personnel should have an idea of what to look for to identify students who belong. They are sometimes identifiable by special colors, clothing, hair styles, insignias, graffiti marks, gestures, or code words. As a way of discouraging gang fights on school property, administrators and

Table 2.2 Crisis Management

The following information is helpful in organizing a crisis management plan.

Form a committee of school personnel, parents, health professionals, social service professionals, and emergency personnel to develop a school crisis management plan.

The committee should address all possible crises and recommend specific steps for preparation.

Have the committee develop a checklist outlining the procedures and responsibilities in the event of a crisis. The checklist shows who is responsible for certain activities: for example, making telephone calls to emergency and community agencies, notifying school personnel with first-aid training, announcing the special code word to alert faculty and staff, disseminating prewritten form letters to parents, and meeting with the press.

Arrange for the committee to compile a crisis information packet and conduct a workshop session for school personnel. During the session, review the emergency plan, explain the notification system, assign responsibilities, and identify procedures to keep faculty, students, parents, and the media informed.

SOURCE: Adapted from Kadel and Follman (1993) and Lichtenstein, Schonfeld, and Kline (1994).

safety officers should know and talk with gang members about the consequences of violence. Any rumors or reports of possible racial or gang fights among students should be taken seriously (California State Department of Education, 1989).

Also, the employee background check is a safe-school employment practice. The personnel office has to ensure that no one with a history of violent criminal behavior or an arrest record for sex-related crimes (sexual assault, child molestation) is granted employment. In some school districts, employees are also tested for drug use and investigated for major infractions against their driver's license (check your state laws).

Another safety feature is to prepare school employees to respond quickly to a crisis situation using a systematic plan to start action when notified (see Table 2.2). As part of the plan, faculty and staff are trained for specific roles and know how to react in an emergency situation (e.g., natural disasters, shootings, accidents).

If no school crisis management plan or notification system is currently available, the planning process can begin by organizing a comprehensive crisis intervention team. School employees, along with representatives from community health agencies, social service agencies, and emergency organizations, should be members of the team. They can assist with efforts to develop a crisis response plan, provide crisis response training, and maintain a state of readiness to deal with unexpected emergencies.

These suggestions for a safe school are proactive and prevention-oriented measures (Lichtenstein, Schonfield, & Kline, 1994), with the understanding that policies, goals, and procedures differ among schools. School leaders should allow their personnel the freedom to adjust and adapt ideas to ensure students a secure environment.

A Peaceable Environment

Educators interested in constructing a peaceable environment continuously examine school effectiveness and identify areas for improvement. A sample examination can start right now. Identify a school and ask the following questions about its environment:

- Does the school have an orderly environment?
- Does the school promote an academic emphasis?
- Are there expectations for success?

Now, ask two more questions:

- Are models of appropriate behaviors, attitudes, and beliefs encouraged by the school's climate?
- Have faculty and staff developed a consensus on a code of conduct and consistent enforcement?

These questions appear in the literature on effective schools research (Squires, 1980). Throughout the literature, one significant criterion for effective schools is a safe and orderly environment, revealing the importance of having a calm learning atmosphere. It recognizes the need for cooperation and agrees with the qualities Sweeney (1983) recommends for a healthy climate.

1. Cohesiveness—the degree to which everyone is able to work together to solve problems.
2. Expectations—the degree to which high expectations are communicated for both adults and students.

3. Esprit—the feeling of satisfaction and loyalty among school personnel.
4. Goal orientation—the sense of direction shared by the faculty and staff.
5. Leadership—successfully getting everyone to work together toward the same goals.

Does the environment at your school possess the qualities listed? Is it an emotionally positive setting—one in which individuals are surrounded by harmonious attitudes, behaviors, and channels of communication? Does it reinforce the priorities of academic achievement and scholastic success for all students?

In responding to the questions, you know the degree to which your school represents a peaceable environment, one that appeals favorably to the human senses: what you see, feel, taste, touch, hear, and smell. Overall, it should be a place where there is equal treatment for everyone and no evidence of emotional, verbal, physical, or destructive violence.

Selling the School

Drive by several schools in different neighborhoods and ask yourself the following questions:

1. What do I like about the school?
2. What do I dislike about the school?

Then look at your school from the perspective of trying to sell it to a real estate agent. Do the facilities reflect personal pride, physical attractiveness, and upkeep? Are the grounds neat and clean? Is there appropriate use of space and equipment? A school's appearance is the first indicator that students and school personnel maintain an interest in the building. School environment questions in Table 2.3 can help you further assess the interior and exterior features.

If a school resembles a fortress, it may give the distinct impression that control is the main objective. Sometimes security measures affect the school's appearance and increase the apprehensions of students and faculty (e.g., boarded windows, high fences, locked

Table 2.3 School Environment Questions

---

1. Is your school building attractive?
2. What would you recommend to make the school more attractive?
3. When entering your classroom in the morning, what is your first impression?
4. Do you enjoy being inside the school building during the day?
5. When exiting the building at the close of the school day, what is your last impression?
6. Are entrances and exits clearly marked for safety?
7. Does traffic flow create a bottleneck or overcrowded conditions at certain times during the day (e.g., classes changing, students entering building, or lunch periods)?
8. Are hallways, locker rooms, restrooms, and stairwells free of obstructions, properly lighted, and adequately supervised?
9. Is there adequate space for students to play indoors during inclement weather?
10. Do the school halls and corridors allow for easy monitoring of students and visitors?
11. Can visitors enter the building or classrooms without stopping at the office for approval?
12. Are doors to storage spaces, equipment rooms, basements, and attics locked?

---

doors, and safety checkpoints for entry and exit). When a school looks like a place for incarceration both inside and outside, it is imperative that the internal climate be changed to exhibit warmth, color, brightness, and cleanliness.

Old schools, regardless of location (urban, suburban, or rural), are unappealing when they need major repairs. Kozol (1991) reports that schools in poor urban neighborhoods are literally falling apart. He describes a conversation with a principal who told him the following:

> One classroom . . . has been sealed off because of a gaping hole in the floor. In the band room, chairs are positioned where acoustic tiles don't fall quite so often. Plaster and ceramic tile have peeled off the walls, leaving the external brick wall of the school exposed. (p. 100)

This deteriorating building sounds like a forsaken, unpleasant refuge. Students and personnel cannot be satisfied with the appearance of their school.

A school that looks like a mall, a library, a restaurant, or a conference center and less like an abandoned institution will have an environment more conducive to learning (U.S. Department of Education, 1988). Students and teachers prefer a spacious and positive environment as opposed to crowded rooms and halls.

The physical condition of a school, whether new or old, will influence the desire of people to be there. Also, consider what makes it attractive—location, property value, visibility, or a curbside appeal. They are the same features buyers consider when purchasing a home. If you are not proud of the building, then these questions should come to mind:

What kind of repairs are needed?
Who can help solve the problems?

Making the Classroom Peaceable

Think of a classroom where the teacher is firm about keeping order, but is unable to manage hostile behavior. Imagine sparks flying through the air as he or she is determined to stop disruptions. Then, one day disruptive student behavior turns into serious fighting, and the sparks multiply into rapidly burning flames.

The flames turn into a roaring fire requiring tons of water. When the fire is out, students are quiet but there is no peace.

So, what is a peaceable classroom?

A peaceable classroom is where the teacher and students work as a warm and caring community. Five qualities identify the various peacemaking skills and behaviors taught within such an environment (Kreidler, 1984, p. 3).

1. *Cooperation.* Students learn to work together and trust, help, and share with each other.
2. *Communication.* Students learn to observe carefully, communicate accurately, and listen sensitively.
3. *Tolerance.* Students learn to respect and appreciate people's differences and to understand prejudice and how it works.
4. *Positive Emotional Expression.* Students learn to express feelings, particularly anger and frustration, in ways that are not aggressive or destructive, and they learn self-control.

Table 2.4 Classroom Environment Inventory

Directions: Check "Yes" or "No" for each item.

Yes	No	
___	___	1. Are classrooms organized to accommodate student-centered learning?
___	___	2. Are classrooms attractively decorated, and are materials properly displayed?
___	___	3. Do classrooms have sufficient space for group as well as individual work?
___	___	4. Do classroom seating arrangements prevent students from disturbing one another when entering or exiting the room?
___	___	5. Do classrooms have the needed supplies, equipment, and resources for teaching and learning?
___	___	6. Do classroom rules include clear expectations and guidelines for student behavior?
___	___	7. Do the classrooms have adequate chalkboard and bulletin board space?
___	___	8. Do classrooms have adequate heating, lighting, and ventilation?
___	___	9. Do classrooms have enough space for the teacher and students to move easily about the room?
___	___	10. Do classrooms present the image that school is a safe and peaceful place in which to learn?

---

5. *Conflict Resolution.* Students learn the skills of responding creatively to conflict in the context of a supportive, caring environment.

A classroom should have sufficient space for students to learn and practice these peacemaking skills. The teacher might arrange the furniture in a circle or U-shape to observe and interact with students. Ample space provides easy access to the pencil sharpener, resources, and supplies, and prevents students from disturbing others.

An inspection of the room, using the classroom environment inventory (Table 2.4), can help identify areas where changes or improvements are needed. Checking to determine whether students are comfortable in the seating arrangement is important. Students need to sit where they can actively participate, see the chalkboard, and move easily around the room.

Also a teacher should question old practices as new practices evolve. According to Drew (1987), the person changes, compromises, and leaves old habits behind. In her book, Drew identifies peaceable classrooms as environments where teachers foster the commitment to have a better world. She states, "Dealing with discipline, resolving conflicts, affirming each child's value, and pointing out his or her connections to the world forms the base for a commitment to peace" (Preface, p. 2).

The base Drew (1987) refers to develops in a setting where students learn to work collaboratively, solve problems, and possess the ability to say, "I'm human, I'll make mistakes, and I'll try again."

What Causes Conflict?

Any environment where hostile or aggressive students use weapons to solve disputes is unsafe. The federal government has taken steps to ensure that some of the causes of conflict and fear be removed from schools. It enacted a goal that school employees, peace officers, parents, and community members should work to fulfill. The goal states: "Every school in the United States will be free of drugs, violence, and the unauthorized presence of firearms and alcohol, and will offer a disciplined environment" (U.S. Department of Education, 1991). Thus every classroom should be a violence-free setting where order is maintained.

Initiatives to achieve this national goal have progressed with the understanding that the causes of conflict are many. In some classrooms, the conflicts are attributed to

1. a competitive atmosphere,
2. an intolerant atmosphere,
3. poor communication,
4. inappropriate expression of emotion,
5. lack of conflict resolution skills, or
6. a misuse of power by the teacher. (Kreidler, 1984, pp. 4-5)

In describing these conflicts, a competitive atmosphere is obviously one in which students display the attitude that only winners count and everyone looks out for him- or herself. As for unfriendly students who mistreat, resent, or hate each other, their negative actions create an intolerant learning atmosphere. Such antisocial behaviors deflate positive attitudes as the teacher tries to encourage everyone to learn.

The classroom climate suffers from poor communication when students misunderstand or misperceive the intentions, feelings, needs, or actions of others. It is important for them to share emotions and feelings without using aggression to express anger and frustration. Students lacking skills in anger management and self-control cause continual behavioral problems with their inappropriate expressions of emotion. Also, when students have no conflict resolution or peer mediation skills, contentions and disputes are resolved only for short periods and will recur later.

Occasionally, teachers have to assume direct responsibility for discipline problems and classroom conflicts, especially if they (a) set a multitude of inflexible rules, (b) harshly criticize the class, (c) establish irrational or impossibly high academic standards, (d) use a biased grading system, or (e) display frightening mood swings. The power and authority exercised by teachers are critical factors in the positive and negative behaviors of students. In handling serious conflicts among students, teachers should receive assistance from school administrators, support staff, and parents.

Classroom Management and Discipline

A teacher's repertoire of classroom management techniques requires continual renewal in an effort to achieve and maintain a peaceable classroom. The renewal is possible through professional development sessions, which introduce functional ideas and practical techniques on managing student misbehavior, empowering the teacher to integrate and adjust new methods to his or her class.

There is no "one size fits all" classroom management approach. Teachers reluctant to alter their methods will probably resist (a) refining or changing classroom management and discipline approaches, (b) learning new discipline approaches to help modify the student referral process, and (c) asking colleagues who possess exemplary discipline techniques to share useful ideas.

It's true that some behavior management techniques are fads and trendy ideas. They work for a few days or until students find ways to undermine them. Teachers will have to try many techniques with the understanding that some will be effective and others will not. The most common technique in use, regardless of fads, is the *obedience* approach. Students are told to follow the rules, and if they disobey, punishment is used to keep them in line.

Then there is the approach that allows students to reflect on their misconduct, explain the causes, and decide how to behave without breaking the rules; it is called the *responsibility* model (Curwin & Mendler, 1988). In this model, students are taught the positive and negative consequences of their behavior and they get to make choices on how to behave. Another model that focuses on positive action is the *catch them being good* approach—the method of acknowledging students in the act of doing something right (Drew, 1987).

The recent no-nonsense discipline approach referred to as the *zero-tolerance* approach (U.S. Department of Education, 1993) is intended to discourage school violence through long-term suspension or expulsion. In some schools, this approach includes a parent-student contract in which students agree not to participate in violent activities or cause disruptions. If students violate the contract by fighting or bringing deadly weapons or drugs to school, their enrollment is terminated immediately.

During the period of termination, students should not be home alone with free time to commit criminal or violent acts in the community. Although school districts handle terminations differently, special programs or provisions are needed to occupy the time of suspended or expelled students. An innovative idea might be a "no frill, no thrill" school where they study self-control and violence prevention.

Other discipline approaches designed to address behavioral problems are listed in the appendix. Whatever approach is used, it should be appropriate for both the school and the community. For example, afterschool detention for misbehaved students would be inappropriate in a community where the school bus schedule does not include an afterschool bus route.

Sound discipline practices contribute to good conduct and academic achievement, as these elements go together in successful schools (U.S. Department of Education, 1986). For this reason, effective teaching and the enforcement of conduct codes by faculty are essential. The faculty and staff should feel satisfied making decisions to prevent, intervene, or resolve antisocial behavior. In addition, they need the assurance that administrators will support their classroom management decisions.

Closing Thoughts

This chapter concludes with two additional perspectives for you to consider—*culture* and *economic cost.* Regarding culture, there is a plausible argument confronting efforts to create a secure environment without addressing ethnicity.

"A 'safe' [and peaceful] environment in schools where all children can learn is unattainable without addressing cultural and ethnic factors" (Gay, 1994, p. 142).

The school and home behaviors students display are no doubt influenced and motivated by culture. For this reason, the development of ethnic pride and identity as part of the educational enterprise is critical. If a peaceful atmosphere is what we want for children, then a commitment to recognize their ethnicity and cultural experiences deserves more attention.

Creating a peaceable environment that includes ethnic factors strengthens the mission for children to live and learn in harmony. In working to achieve this mission, educators could conceivably reduce the revenue spent on violence. Besides, there are individuals who argue, "This nation should not consider the human loss, not to mention property damage, we annually suffer from crime and violence in our schools as an acceptable cost in educating our children" (Rapp, Carrington, & Nicholson, 1992).

The financial costs, as well as the elimination of life, are causes for alarm at a time when communities and parents expect quality education for their tax dollar. We need their help in creating safe and orderly surroundings for students to learn.

Let's Talk

1. How can a principal set the tone for a peaceable school environment?
2. If you had the opportunity, what would you do to change the interior and exterior of schools?
3. In your opinion, what can teachers do to create a peaceable classroom?
4. How can students help maintain a safe and orderly classroom?

5. What strategies would you recommend to help schools assess and revise their code of conduct?

6. What are your ideas on explaining the need for a crisis management plan to children?

Suggested Activities

1. Outline ways to achieve a peaceable school environment and share it with school administrators.

2. Plan and decorate a colorful hallway bulletin board using peace as the theme.

3. Organize a group to develop or revise a school crisis management plan. As part of the plan, conduct a training workshop and disseminate the information needed for an unexpected crisis.

4. Use the school and classroom environment questions in this chapter to develop a survey to determine what faculty and staff like and dislike about your school's atmosphere. Get approval to administer the survey, analyze the data, and report the findings to school personnel for their feedback.

5. Organize a school-community group to plan and sponsor a safe school poetry, slogan, or poster contest. Give prizes to the winners and display the winning entries throughout the school.

Learning Exercises

The following exercises are specific ideas to help teachers create a trusting and caring environment for students.

1. Select two "Students of the Week" (male and female) chosen for their hobbies, humor, creativity, future aspirations, or personal accomplishments.

2. Have students follow teachers, support staff, or administrators during the day. When the students return to class, have them tell classmates what they observed during the shadowing experience.

3. Have students prepare a time capsule of school life for the future.

4. Have students write a new school song in which success, motivation, and peace are key components.

5. Have students be pen pals or start a classroom newsletter exchange.

6. Have students serve as mentors and tutors for younger or new students.

7. Help students identify a project that they can complete as a gift to the school (e.g., restoring torn library books, cleaning physical education equipment, or picking up litter).

8. Have students prepare and hang an attractive poster listing the qualities of a peaceful classroom.

9. Have students create a community service project (i.e., a neighborhood beautification program) in which they learn civic responsibility.

10. Have students create bulletin boards and murals depicting positive aspects of life in school.

11. Encourage recognition of special days in the lives of students such as birthdays, passing the driver's exam, athletic accomplishments, and academic honors.

12. Organize a "You Have a Friend Day" for students to get to know one another.

PRINCIPLE 3

The dynamics of communication should build interactive relationships and the peaceful exchange of feelings, decisions, and ideas.

~ 3 ~

Encouraging Peaceful Communication

There is no pleasure to me without communication; there is not so much as a sprightly thought comes into my mind but I grieve that I have no one to tell it to.

                                                                Montaigne

What kind of impression do youngsters receive when they observe communication among peers and adults? When observing communicative relationships, do we see people being peaceful, respectful, and tolerant of others? Most people learn positive and negative informational exchanges by interacting with one another. Although interactions vary, communication should be inclusive and encourage individuals to do the following:

- Share information with others willingly
- Listen and respond peacefully during the exchange of information
- Go beyond the first impression of others to develop a communicative relationship

Inclusive communication allows all parties to engage in power sharing, reflection, negotiation, encouragement, and clarification. The focus is a peaceful "win-win" situation in which everyone brings

Table 3.1 Different Forms of Communication

Experiences	Categories	Actions
Feelings		
Attitudes	Emotional	Joy, anger,
Apprehensions	communication	fear
Ideas		
Knowledge	Intellectual	Study, read,
Imagination	communication	reflect
Movements		
Body language	Physical	Posture, gestures,
Health-wellness	communication	eye statements
Relationships		
Verbal language	Interpersonal	Voice, speech,
Social interaction	communication	etiquette
Lifestyles		
Kinship	Cultural	Ethnic music,
Identity	communication	stories, rituals

ideas to the table, learns to listen to opposing views, and draws conclusions on courses of action. No one is viewed as having exclusive rights to workable solutions. A peaceful exchange of information affirms the rights and responsibilities of others and breaks down barriers to understanding.

Forms of Communication

We possess the capacity to transmit information through emotional, intellectual, physical, interpersonal, and cultural communication. Human experiences and actions within the different categories of communication are identified in Table 3.1 and followed by an enumeration.

Emotional Communication

Everyone likes the joy of happy emotions such as excitement and laughter, and they contribute to lower stress and relaxation. On occasion, these emotions are criticized by individuals who say, "If you are having fun, you are not working" and "If you are laughing, you are not learning." Sadly, these negative responses to joyous behavior can cause adults and children to conceal their feelings.

When no emotional outlets exist, individuals can suffer from suppressed anxieties. They may feel powerless, unwilling to expose the true self, or reluctant to express thoughts. Another apprehension is the uncertainty individuals face in teaching youngsters. For example, school personnel can experience an uneasiness in trying to reach and excite the cognitive modalities through which each child learns best. In attempting to acknowledge the individuality of each child, Paley (1979) says the following:

> The challenge in teaching is to find a way of communicating to each child the idea that his or her special quality is understood, is valued, and can be talked about. It is not easy, because we are influenced by the fears and prejudices, apprehensions and expectations, which have become a carefully hidden part of every one of us. (p. xv)

Naturally, you might ask, What kind of feelings, attitudes, and apprehensions do adults hide? Can they be successful in concealing their emotions from children? Actually, children recognize the feelings people express (e.g., joy, apathy, pain). They know which emotions receive attention and which emotions should be disguised to avoid punishment (e.g., laughing, crying, screaming).

We disclose many feelings, but the downside of emotional communication is anger and verbal abuse. Whenever individuals make offensive remarks, they depreciate the feelings of others and devalue self-worth. A school that emphasizes peace among faculty, staff members, and students will teach anger management techniques to help defuse negative emotions.

For instance, we know that violent rage is an extreme emotion. When a person is enraged and communication is impossible, it could mean making a choice between fight or flight. Think about the choices you have made. Then, analyze the escalation of emotion before, during, and after a serious disagreement or fight with someone. At what point could you have stopped yourself? When did you think about the consequences?

Intellectual Communication

The intellectual process of learning involves making a connection between what one learns and what one knows. During the connection, a person revises and expands his or her thinking—two important features of intellectual communication.

According to Caine and Caine (1991), critical thinking and reflection in learning are not simple processes. Students need time to explore changes in learning and to ask such questions as "What did I do?" "Why did I do it?" and "What did I learn?" Teaching them how to reflect through deliberate strategies can broaden their natural inclination to learn from mistakes and impulsive behavior.

Several intellectually oriented activities for school personnel to consider for use with students are suggested by School and Cooper (1986).

Verbal Rehearsal. This is a query into one's actions for the person to think aloud. The teacher, for example, questions the action of a student who hits a classmate with a book. During the questioning, the teacher describes the behavior and asks the student to stop and think about what he or she did to the classmate. Then, the student explains aloud the inappropriateness of the misbehavior.

Visual Imagery. This is the use of imagination for a person to decide how he or she will act in a conflict situation. The teacher asks students to close their eyes and visualize how they might apologize to someone for inappropriate conduct and what they plan to do differently in the future. In addition, the students could role play and summarize their points of view on resolving the conflict peacefully.

Verbal Analogy. This is a way to connect a person's imagination to an idea, place, or situation. A teacher might say to the class, "Remember when we visited the zoo? We saw owls that did not move. Well, let's act like the owls and not move for a few seconds."

Reflective Thinking Checklist. This is a list of items for students to complete or think about each week. The following are some examples of items teachers might use on a checklist.

- Have I been helpful to other members of the class?

- Do I need to forgive someone for his or her actions?
- Do I need to thank someone for being thoughtful or kind to me?

Teaching students to think logically and constructively develops their intellectual communication skills. They gain the ability to imagine life without violence and what they must do to stay away from persons who commit crimes. In thinking about alternatives and learning not to act on sudden impulses, youngsters may be more inclined to consider their other choices.

Physical Communication

The movements of individuals walking, standing, and running represent nonverbal actions. They are aspects of physical communication, which also includes facial movements, eye statements, and posture. School faculty and staff can obtain an informative playback of their movements by asking students to perform imitations. Everyone should maintain a sense of humor and not feel threatened by students demonstrating the movements they see most often.

Depending on the grade level, the nonverbal actions of hugging and touching will vary. Children either like or dislike being touched on the shoulder, head, or arm by adults. In fact, faculty members may have concerns about placing their hands on students; they may be hesitant about physical contact for fear children might misinterpret their intentions.

Despite the preferences regarding touching, other nonverbal actions can be used to accept and direct student behavior. In reading the nonverbal cues listed in Table 3.2, see if they include some of your physical gestures.

When nonverbal cues from teachers are clearly understood by students, they may provide uninterrupted time for practice or independent seat work. Nonverbal movements can be useful silent signals in guiding the performance of students.

Another aspect of physical communication is body image, the appearance of health and wellness. Remember, people who know you might see when you are not well or preoccupied with other thoughts. The messages from physical communication can convey images of you being energetic, motivated, weak, sleepy, or tired.

Table 3.2 Teacher Nonverbal Cues

---

1. *Accepts student behavior.* Smiles, affirmatively shakes head, pats on the back, winks, places hand on shoulder or arm.
2. *Praises student behavior.* Places index finger and thumb together, claps, raises eyebrows and smiles, nods head approvingly and smiles.
3. *Displays students' ideas.* Writes comments on board, puts students' work on bulletin board, holds up papers, provides for nonverbal student demonstrations, plans mimic role play activities.
4. *Shows interest in student behavior.* Establishes and maintains eye contact.
5. *Moves to facilitate student-to-student interaction.* Physically moves into the position of group member or physically moves away from the group.
6. *Gives directions to students.* Points with the hand or silent movement of lips, looks at specified area, employs predetermined signal (such as raising hands for students to stand up), reinforces numerical aspects by showing number of fingers, extends arms forward and beckons with the hands, points to students for answers.
7. *Shows authority toward students.* Frowns, stares, raises eyebrows, taps foot, negatively shakes head, walks or looks away from the deviant, snaps fingers.
8. *Focuses students' attention on important points.* Uses pointer, walks toward the person or object, taps on something, thrusts head forward, thrusts arm forward, employs a nonverbal movement with a verbal statement to give it emphasis.
9. *Demonstrates, illustrates, or both.* Performs a physical skill, manipulates materials and media, illustrates a verbal statement with a nonverbal action.
10. *Ignores student behavior.* Lacks nonverbal response when one is ordinarily expected. (Sometimes this cue is an appropriate classroom management technique.)

SOURCE: Adapted from Love and Roderick (as cited in Cooper, 1988).

Interpersonal Communication

Words, statements, and comments expressed verbally in conversation among individuals are elements of interpersonal communication. Take a moment to ponder what schools would be like without verbal communication. As the knowers and givers of information, educators articulate their knowledge for students to learn through oral language and social interaction. A teacher who decided to explore language with her students tells this story.

In the midst of [class] discussion, Louis asked one of his characteristically exasperating questions: "But where do words come from . . . ? I stumbled over an answer. . . .

—What use are words anyway?

—Why do people have to talk?

—Why are there good words and bad words?

—Why aren't you supposed to use some words in class?

—Why can't you change words as you like?

I felt that I was being "put on," and was tempted to pass over the questions glibly; there were no simple answers to the children's questions, and the simplest thing to do when children ask difficult questions is to pretend that they're not serious or they're stupid. But the children were serious.

More and more they asked about language and would not be put off by evasive references to the past, linguistic convention, and tradition. Children look away from adults as soon as adults say that things are the way they are because they have always been that way. When a child accepts such an answer, it is a good indication that he has given up and decided to be what adults would make him rather than himself.

I decided to explore language with the children. (Kohl, 1967, pp. 19-20)

The decision that confronted this teacher occurred a generation ago. Still, it could be any teacher today trying to satisfy the students' need for answers to their questions. In fulfilling the learners' quest for knowledge, verbal messages telling them to appreciate their own talent are important.

Positive verbal behaviors are unlikely to erode anyone's self-esteem or hinder the freedom to communicate. However, be sensitive to the fact that a person's autonomy can be expanded or limited by communicative behavior. Specific behaviors that increase and decrease interpersonal communication are mentioned here (Schmuck & Runkel, 1985, pp. 98-99).

Increase Interpersonal Communication

—Listen attentively rather than merely remaining silent

—Use paraphrasing to check your impression of the person's inner state

—Seek information to understand the person

—Offer information relevant to the person's concern

—Describe observable behaviors that influence you

—Directly report your own feelings

—Offer your opinions or state your position

Decrease Interpersonal Communication

—Change the subject without explanation
—Interpret the person's behavior by describing unchangeable experiences or qualities
—Advise and persuade the person
—Vigorously agree with an "I told you so" or obligate the person with a "How could you?" statement
—Approve or urge the person to conform to your standards
—Claim to know what motivates the person's behavior
—Make a command

The use of certain actions to acknowledge, interact, and extend friendship to another person starts with open communication. If you have the ability to generate more cooperation at your school, then begin by supporting individuals willing to foster interpersonal communication among students and adults.

Cultural Communication

School is the one place where we come in contact with cultural communication. People convey cultural differences by expressing themselves through dance, music, stories, and traditions. These expressions draw on *kinship* and *identity,* two meaningful aspects of culture. Kinship is the membership of people in a family, group, or partnership with a common connection based on social relations, heritage, or background.

Identity refers to the distinct characteristics of an individual as well as the characteristics others perceive or believe about the person. For example, a teacher might tell a child, "Your sisters made the honor roll, and I expect the same of you." This child is perceived as a high achiever because her academic identity is predetermined by the performance of older siblings.

Ethnic identity relates to nationality, race, and culture. It is distinguishable by characteristics that correspond to "different ways of valuing, being and behaving" (Gay, 1994, p. 78). Identity also includes bodily features, a person's physical size, complexion, and hair.

In total, cultural communication portrays the essence of people along the lines of their ethnic traits and behaviors.

Communication Among School Personnel

How can communication among educators be extended to include more collegial interaction? Typically, "[teachers] talk about the tasks they perform, the methods they use to get tasks accomplished, . . . [but] rarely, their relations with one another" (Schmuck & Runkel, 1985, p. 93). When do school employees shift from educational concerns to personal concerns? Encouraging people to start communicative exchanges by talking about themselves can uncover skills and talents seldom revealed in school.

Think about building communication among administrators, faculty, and staff members through the establishment of a skills information network. It might be organized as a resource data bank using various channels of communication: telephone, correspondence, publications, electronic mail, and word of mouth. Any communicative network that brings the school community closer together with the intent of enriching the personal and professional sides of life is useful.

With open communication, matters affecting faculty and staff are brought to the principal's attention. This gives them an opportunity to respond before action is taken to make decisions. When such an opportunity is not provided or disallowed, it causes dissatisfaction. The scenario that follows is an example of how a dissatisfied faculty reacted when told what to do.

Immediately following an afterschool faculty meeting, several teachers gathered in the parking lot to express their discontent with the zero-tolerance discipline procedure. According to them, school officials chose to attack the students and not the problem, plus they resented the additional paperwork.

During the faculty meeting, a teacher voiced his unhappiness with the discipline procedure. The principal responded abruptly, "You teachers must complete the paperwork; violence is out of control and I plan to deal with it in a swift,

*no-nonsense manner." He continued to explain, "The paper-
work is required for the file in the case of a lawsuit."*

---

*When another teacher spoke out, questioning her legal rights
and responsibilities in preparing the paperwork, the principal
commented, "Don't complain, be flexible." Extremely upset,
the teacher sat down and refused to establish eye contact with
anyone during the remainder of the meeting. The person sitting next to her murmured, "We've always been told what
to do, whether it made sense or not."*

---

*As the teachers continued their conversation in the parking
lot, the principal drove by. They didn't wave good-bye, making
their dissatisfaction obvious.*

The teachers at this school felt defeated by the "I know what's
best for you" syndrome. They had major concerns about the problem
being presented as their responsibility. In cases in which solutions to
problems come from an authoritarian figure, the faculty may feel no
responsibility for making them work and may even work to make
them fail (Wayson et al., 1982). A reduction in the frustration ex-
perienced by faculty and staff members is critical to the process of
building peaceful communication.

Changing Negative Communication

Violent musical lyrics, videos, and television programs set the
norms for negative communication. The media desensitizes children
to violence, abusive language, and destruction (Carlsson-Paige &
Levin, 1992). They learn to use verbal and physical power as pressure
tactics in gaining recognition. Such hostile behavior is translated into
words and statements that control, degrade, or intimidate others. In
an effort to change negative communication, ask yourself,

---

*What can I do to prevent the students' use of negative
language?*

Table 3.3 Student Communication Inventory

Directions: Check "Yes" or "No" for each item.

Yes	No	
___	___	1. Do students listen to the person who is speaking?
___	___	2. Do students think about ideas from the speakers' perspective?
___	___	3. Does each student get a turn to speak?
___	___	4. Do students interrupt while you or others are speaking?
___	___	5. Do students make negative comments about other students?
___	___	6. Do students work out their verbal disputes and disagreements nonviolently?
___	___	7. Do you listen carefully to what students have to say?
___	___	8. Do students have to get your permission before they can speak?
___	___	9. Do you allow students enough time to explain thoughts and ideas clearly?
___	___	10. Do you agree to repeat information when students tell you they don't understand?
___	___	11. Do you allow students opportunities to talk about things of interest to them?
___	___	12. Do you thank students for sharing their ideas and opinions?

One suggestion is to serve as a mentor. Spend time modeling positive language use and teaching students to communicate properly in public places. Another suggestion is to create phrases to replace profanity, for example: "Go to __ell" becomes "Go to the mall" and "Oh, s__it" becomes "Oh, sugar." Also, consider organizing extracurricular seminars for students on proper etiquette and public speaking. Good communication and social skills will prepare them for career success.

Next, ask yourself,

How might I help students get to know and understand one another?

You can begin by realizing the importance students place on peer acceptance and approval. They want to be accepted by their friends and feel liked as a member of the group. In helping them get to know others, make it possible for them to listen and interact with individuals who have different lifestyles, aspirations, and outlooks on life. Use the student communication inventory (Table 3.3) to audit and think about your communicative transactions with students.

While at school, students need to see adults address colleagues in a pleasant tone of voice, extend daily greetings, and smile when they encounter each other. Such transactions display common courtesy and peaceful communication. However, students who lack training in the social graces may not equate politeness with respect. They need to understand and practice social etiquette in a way that empowers them to interact and express themselves in a positive manner.

The Language of Peace

Children and adults promote the language of peace when they practice the use of phrases such as "thank-you," "excuse me," "please," "pardon me," "good morning," "good afternoon," "ladies and gentlemen," "quiet, please," "it is good to see you today," "please go first," and "welcome" when encountering another person. By having these phrases prominently displayed around the school building, the students' exposure to common courtesies is increased.

Another means of emphasizing peaceful language is to set a standard of "no put-downs." A put-down can be, "Yuck, gross!" said about another child's lunch, a racial or ethnic slur, or a "no girls allowed" comment (Thomson, 1993, p. 13). To address the problem, give students examples of what their put-downs are, then explain how the comments hurt the feelings of others. Also, sexual harassment policies have been enforced in some school districts. Students are warned about taunting remarks, sexual advances, and unwelcome touching. To prevent harassment, the faculty and staff members should set aside time to talk with students about the use of dirty words, rude statements, and sexually explicit phrases.

Collective decisions on developing the activities needed to promote decent communication and sensitivity toward discrimination are necessary. Students should hear positive language from adults and practice it among their peers, engage in meaningful discussions, and learn to express themselves clearly. Unfortunately, the labels used for identification purposes in education stigmatize individuals. Certain children are referred to as *disadvantaged, inner-city, at-risk, culturally deprived, poverty-stricken, minority, remedial,* or *handicapped.* They are viewed as different and can even be perceived as inferior by others. Having to tolerate the insensitivity of their peers, these children should not have to create defensive mechanisms or survival tactics against the stereotypic terms used to identify them in school.

The generous aspect of communication is the use of an individual's name. No one wants to be treated like a number or an object occupying space as when addressed as "Hey, you." Greetings and introductions by name seem formal, but the formality acknowledges a person properly. Such practices strengthen the language of peace by valuing the use of communication to honor each other.

Identifying Communication Styles

What kind of communication style do you recommend or use with students?

Communication style refers to a person's ability to apply dynamic energy as a speaker, maintain the listener's attention, and manipulate the mood of an audience (Cooper, 1988). These three forms of interaction affect the way students learn, perform, and behave. Other communication elements that affect learning are mentioned in the various teacher communication styles and interactive patterns described in Table 3.4.

Differences between communication styles range from productive to unproductive professional behavior. Unproductive activity impedes the instructional process when it restricts teacher-student interaction—particularly if a teacher threatens the class with maintaining order on a regular basis. Any time expressions become unfriendly or demanding, valuable instructional time is wasted telling students how to behave.

When the school year starts, students will watch and study a teacher's communication style carefully. It takes a while for them to become accustomed to the teacher's intentional and unintentional messages. Once familiar with the communication style, they can usually predict how the teacher will react in certain situations.

Another aspect of communication style includes listening—the element of understanding the needs, aspirations, and problems of individuals. Misinterpretations and distortions can occur when people fail to listen to or understand what others are saying. A good listener focuses on the speaker's perceived problem or need without giving immediate solutions.

The main objective of a skillful listener is to give the speaker an opportunity to think about possible solutions or alternatives to a

Table 3.4 Teacher Communication Styles

---

1. *Directive.* The teacher is demanding, sets high standards, dominates class discussion, and expects students to complete their work.
2. *Authoritative.* The teacher is enthusiastic, develops well-planned and logically structured lessons with various instructional techniques, and shows a personal interest in students.
3. *Tolerant and Authoritative.* The teacher forms a close relationship with students, concentrates on teaching, ignores minor disruptions, organizes activities for small group work, and allows for student responsibility and freedom.
4. *Tolerant.* The teacher fails to challenge students academically, has poorly prepared lessons, lacks academic expectations, but does show an interest in the personal lives of students.
5. *Uncertain-Tolerant.* The teacher assumes little leadership in an unstructured class, ignores students' inattentiveness at times, and students don't know what to expect when the teacher does react to misbehavior.
6. *Uncertain-Aggressive.* The teacher does not explain rules properly; overreacts to student misbehavior; displays unpredictable, unbalanced, and opponent-type behaviors; and permits confused and aggressive disorder in class.
7. *Repressive.* The teacher may repress students' initiatives through sarcastic remarks, grading system or angry outbursts; lessons are structured but not well organized; and students are uninvolved, docile, and fearful.
8. *Drudging.* The teacher expends a great deal of energy managing the class, does most of the talking, follows a routine, avoids experimenting with new techniques, and looks as if he or she is suffering from work-related burnout.

SOURCE: Adapted from Brekelmans, Levy, and Rodriguez (1993).

problem (Burke, 1995). For example, students need someone who will listen, a sounding board to talk about troubles. When there is no adult listener available to assist them in thinking through problems, students may harm themselves or others.

Effective listening is a time-consuming activity; nevertheless, people listen to enjoy themselves, share information, or understand the feelings of others (Cooper, 1988). In schools these activities remain vital to peaceful interaction among students, faculty, staff, and administrators. They enact the communication styles taught to them as a means of exchanging information and knowledge.

Closing Thoughts

Clearly, the thrust for encouraging peaceful communication is motivated by the actions of people. Specific communicative actions for the reader to consider as the closing thoughts in this chapter are the following *101 Ways to Promote Peace.*

1. Make a new friend.
2. Make a child feel loved.
3. Laugh at yourself.
4. Be safety conscious.
5. Preserve and enjoy nature.
6. Become a mentor and encourage others to do the same.
7. Speak out against intolerance.
8. Write cheerful cards, notes, and letters.
9. Greet visitors with a smile.
10. Do not label people.
11. Be a peaceful role model.
12. Make sincere compliments.
13. Let children know you appreciate them.
14. Organize letter-writing campaigns against injustices.
15. Support programs that assist people.
16. Learn to speak a language that is new to you.
17. Celebrate diversity.
18. Work for human rights.
19. Defend the freedom of expression.
20. Be friendly to neighbors.
21. Be proud of your ethnic identity.
22. Keep a family scrapbook.
23. Be slow to loose your temper.
24. Be a good listener.
25. Use problem-solving skills.
26. Turn frustration into positive action.
27. Be reluctant to criticize others for their mistakes.
28. Teach children to settle disputes without hurling insults.
29. Try to understand why others behave the way they do.
30. Learn to see life through the experiences of others.
31. Listen to different viewpoints.
32. Be considerate of other opinions.
33. Refuse to hit children.
34. Practice good manners.

35. Be respectful and thoughtful.
36. Be courteous to everyone.
37. Condemn dishonesty.
38. Encourage children to try.
39. Share your ideas with others.
40. Do not tolerate hostile behavior from others.
41. Resist making cruel statements.
42. Learn planning and goal-setting skills.
43. Refuse to use vulgar language.
44. Use surprises to make life fun.
45. Object to jokes and stories that ridicule people.
46. Get regular physical checkups, listen to your body.
47. Write letters to suggest ways to improve your community.
48. Organize cultural and social activities.
49. Give to people in need.
50. Teach children how to care for their pets.
51. Take time to do nice things for yourself.
52. Accept changes in your attitudes and feelings.
53. Teach children to tell the truth.
54. Learn to appreciate unique lifestyles.
55. Forgive children for their wrongdoings.
56. Do not underestimate your own abilities.
57. Celebrate holidays and special occasions.
58. Be willing to help others in times of adversity.
59. Count the milestones in your life.
60. Be a trustworthy person.
61. Think before you speak.
62. Take time for your hobbies.
63. Participate in a neighborhood watch group.
64. Teach children to follow the rules when playing games.
65. Serve as a volunteer during your free time.
66. Try to live a peaceful, uncomplicated life.
67. Place your favorite photos in your work area.
68. Perform an act of kindness for someone every day.

69. Invite a foreign student to spend time with your family.
70. Take an interest in the conversations of children.
71. Learn to refuse unacceptable requests politely.
72. Teach children what to do in an emergency.
73. Use a pleasant tone of voice.
74. Show children how to greet peers and adults.
75. Practice good telephone etiquette.
76. Teach children not to damage the property of others.
77. Smile at yourself in the mirror each day.
78. Reflect on peace by writing a poem.
79. Teach children the value of money and work.
80. Learn stress and anger management techniques.
81. Develop healthy eating habits.
82. Make your children happy, let them know you care.
83. Find ways to recognize and honor hardworking people.
84. Refuse to judge people on hearsay evidence.
85. Attend family reunions and gatherings to meet relatives.
86. Do not ignore the fears and phobias of children.
87. Keep your promises.
88. Set achievable objectives.
89. Treat children fairly.
90. Become involved in school-community affairs.
91. Make spending time with children a priority.
92. Learn from the experience of doing something wrong.
93. Use humor to defuse anger and lessen tension.
94. Accentuate positive dreams for the future.
95. Wear comfortable shoes and clothing.
96. Try to stop habits that are bad for your health.
97. Admire the creativity and imagination of others.
98. Be sensitive to matters that can cause conflict.
99. Volunteer to create a family-friendly environment at work.
100. Be an example of inspiration for others to follow.
101. Support the work of peacemakers.

SOURCE: Theresa M. Bey.

Let's Talk

1. What is your opinion about the phrases, remarks, and statements commonly used in school?
2. What kind of communication styles do teachers and parents display?
3. Explain how the information in this chapter caused you to think about your own communication?
4. In your opinion, what kind of verbal and nonverbal communication skills do students need?
5. How can peaceful language increase interaction among students, school personnel, and administrators?
6. What kind of nonverbal cues do you use to accept or direct the actions of another person?

Suggested Activities

1. Present three skits depicting different communication styles. For example, show the interactive patterns of individuals who are (1) self-assured and directive, (2) easygoing and tolerant of others, and (3) repressive. Compare and discuss the skits, then talk about ways to encourage individuals to change unproductive communication styles.
2. Keep a one-week journal of positive and negative personal encounters between people. For each encounter, describe the situation: what was said, what responses or reactions were given, and your impressions. Then, review the journal to determine ways in which the negative encounters could have concluded peacefully or differently.
3. Read "101 Ways to Promote Peace," then list ten (positive) verbal and nonverbal gifts you gave to yourself or to others during a 24-hour period. Gifts can be a smile in the mirror, complimentary phrases, or the completion of an assigned task, for example.
4. Review the scenario in this chapter about teacher dissatisfaction with the zero-tolerance discipline procedure. Analyze

the situation: identify communication problems, possible causes, and actions that might have reduced the frustration.

5. Prepare a list of suggested words and phrases to serve as substitutes for negative terms. The idea is to replace dirty words with decent words for individuals to use. When preparing the list, include ideas from faculty, staff members, and students. Once the list is complete, have them review and accept it as the language of peace.

PRINCIPLE 4

The social curriculum should contain various approaches for students to learn, understand, and accept social responsibility.

❧ 4 ❧

Planning for Peace
Across the Curriculum

*At commencement, graduates are told to go into the world
as peacemakers. Yet in most schools, peace is so unimportant
that no place is found for it in the curriculum.*

McCarthy (1992, p. 6).

When peace is not in the curriculum, faculty and staff miss out on the opportunity of using peacemaking skills to teach core subject matter more effectively. In trying to meet the basic curriculum requirements, school personnel need not worry about peace overshadowing the information currently used in the content areas. This worry is unfounded if the skills and practices of peace are applied as ways to engage students in learning.

In other words, to ensure that required content does not fall through the cracks, faculty and staff can blend subject matter with the real-life context of how to behave peacefully. The blending starts with plans to match formal curriculum resources with the informal experiences of children. Working to eliminate the mismatch between the formal and informal curricula is essential for a peaceable school.

Table 4.1 Curricular Approaches

Subject approach. Curriculum units are organized around separate subject areas or disciplines of knowledge (e.g., literature on female peacemakers, character education, values education).

Broad-fields approach. Curriculum units are organized around concepts related to two or more subjects (e.g., moral ethics in Science and Mathematics, tolerance and peace in American History and World History).

Problems approach. Curriculum units are organized around major social problems (e.g., violence prevention, health problems, drugs, child abuse).

Emerging needs approach. Curriculum units are organized around personal and social needs of learners (e.g., conflict management, social problem solving, social responsibility).

SOURCE: Adapted from Beane and Lipka (1986, p. 95).

What is the best way to plan for peace and nonviolence across the curricula?

First understand that the curriculum is the "content and process by which learners gain knowledge and understanding; develop skills; and alter attitudes, appreciations, and values" (Doll, 1989, p. 8). Therefore, peace can exist as an unrestricted element, limited only by the decisions of people. In making decisions about the content (what one learns) and the process (how one learns), it is necessary for teachers, administrators, and parents to agree on the peacemaking concepts, practices, and skills they want students to use.

Revising the Curriculum

In conducting a review to revise the curriculum, school personnel can start with an assessment of existing content and materials to determine what is currently used to teach peace. During the review, faculty and staff should assess their need to renew existing curricula or obtain new resources (see Appendix). They should also identify models for teaching peace to prevent violence and select the appropriate curricular approach. Several approaches for faculty to consider are listed in Table 4.1.

Once an approach is identified, the faculty and staff members commit to the "process of discovering what knowledge is valuable, why it is valuable, and how it can be acquired" (Schubert, 1986, p. 2).

An effort must be made to link subject matter on peace across grade levels and content areas. For example, nonviolent skills might include anger management in health education, the moral practices of science, crime and the economy in mathematics, motivational songs in music, prosocial vocabulary in language arts, stories about friendships in reading, and protective regulations and laws in social studies.

Changing curricula to help students understand the relevancy of peace requires time—an occupational drawback for busy teachers. At times, the expected and unexpected dilemmas of curriculum modification provide an exceptional opportunity for faculty to alter bland materials and textbook content; especially if the alterations are tailored to fit the learners' interest, knowledge, and ability levels.

The changes in content have to include real-life examples of how peaceful and "positive attitudes allow people to overcome hardships or accomplish great feats" (Marzano et al., 1988, p. 11). A well-structured curriculum helps students understand that attitudes affect behavior and that individuals do have some control over their attitudes.

When social conflicts increase, so do attempts by administrators and teachers to update curriculum materials to defuse the hostile actions of children. Addressing the antisocial behaviors of students through the use of antiweapon, antidrug, and sexual harassment materials is an acceptable practice. Not only is such information important, but children may learn to obey the laws intended for their protection. For these reasons, curricula should contain information that children and youth need to survive. This is a pressing point, because in some crime-ridden communities, students encounter violence every day. This poem makes the point clearly.

> *They hear it, the verbal abuse*
> *They watch it, the defiant behavior*
> *They talk about it, the dishonest intentions*
> *They hurt from it, the mental and physical suffering*
> *They avoid it, the displeasure of staying indoors.*
>
> Theresa M. Bey

Moreover, the violent acts that occur as part of school, home, and neighborhood life argue the need to teach peace across the curricula. Adding peacemaking skills and supporting students' interest in peaceful intervention activities are important to their well-being and safety. A few of the basic peacemaking behaviors they should learn

Table 4.2 Curriculum Review Survey

Directions: Review your school's curriculum program to determine if the following content is included. Circle "Yes" or "No" for each item.

After checking the curriculum, I find that it includes the following:

Yes	No	1. Material about peacemakers and individuals who contribute to the good of society.
Yes	No	2. Content on people who represent various ethnic or racial groups.
Yes	No	3. Information on social skills and social problem-solving techniques.
Yes	No	4. Information on social responsibility along with the principles and values of a democratic society.
Yes	No	5. Strategies that deal with anger management and self-discipline.
Yes	No	6. Content on the moral and ethical issues in all the major subject areas.
Yes	No	7. Obstacles facing the local community, such as economic, political, and social challenges.
Yes	No	8. Materials on peer mediation strategies and conflict resolution skills for students.
Yes	No	9. Content on global communities and international awareness.
Yes	No	10. Information on violence prevention and violence-free alternatives.
Yes	No	11. Content on tolerance and cooperation.
Yes	No	12. Information on gender equity.

---

are cooperation, communication, tolerance, conflict resolution, problem solving, and social responsibility. In checking curriculum to determine the nature and scope of content related to peacemaking, refer to the Curriculum Review Survey, Table 4.2.

The Hidden Curriculum

Aside from the written and planned curriculum, activities produced by unexpected events represent the unplanned curriculum, sometimes referred to as the hidden curriculum. It embraces unintentional "aspects of the learned curriculum that lie outside the boundaries of the school's intentional efforts" (Glatthorn, 1987, p. 20). The unplanned experiences include subtle messages between teachers and learners, behaviors used to cope with the school's bureaucratic organization, and the self-curriculum of motivating one's own self to learn.

Undesirable aspects of the hidden curriculum are evident whenever students hurt their classmates. By fighting, stealing, cheating, or cursing, students disrupt the planned curriculum. In addition, teachers cannot avoid the disorder caused by negative behavior. Some schools, fortunately, have skilled administrators who make a concentrated effort to prevent the annoyances and interruptions caused by unruly students. Otherwise, faculty and staff in poorly supervised schools must learn to cope and develop persistence to withstand an intense unplanned curriculum.

Several examples of unplanned incidents are described in scenes from Howe's book (1991, p. 26-27) in which he discloses his experiences with urban school students.

Scene 1. A student announces, "I can't do my work without a pencil. What do you want me to write with, my finger?" The teacher gives him a pencil and the student says, "No, not a short one. Give me a new one or I'm not working."

Scene 2. A student comes to class late, walks up to a student who is at work, and announces, "Get out of my desk. That is my seat." When the teacher convinces the late student that he has lost his right to his desk by arriving late, the student shoves his work onto the floor and announces, "I'm not working. I don't like this desk, it's too hard."

Scene 3. To the student who finds her book boring, the teacher says, "I was born to bore. I once had a student die of boredom in my classroom."

Scene 4. When a student has been abandoned by his or her entire family, someone will say, "You're so disgusting, your parents don't even want you home on Christmas."

Scene 5. Students constantly label and call out dreadful names. Someone requiring medication to control psychosis will be called a "Thorazine zombie." If a student has dyslexia and is learning disabled, his classmates will ask him to spell "cat" and "dog," and he will be taunted no matter what the answer.

In these scenes, the teacher maintains a controlled temper but does not mention any action to have disruptive students removed from class. Nevertheless, when misconduct reigns in the classroom, teaching the curriculum as intended fails. Such failure may or may not happen often, but a teacher should decide how to respond to the unplanned curriculum in disciplining students for inappropriate behavior. Making a determination about which student behaviors to address or ignore can affect efforts to create a peaceable classroom. Teachers and administrators should give considerable thought to the following questions.

- Do teachers, staff members, and administrators work together to help prevent disruptive student behavior?
- Do teachers and staff members feel comfortable with the current intervention process of handling disruptive student behavior?
- Do teachers feel threatened or fear retribution from students?

In a comparison between the undesired and desired elements of a hidden curriculum, dedicated educators work to accomplish the latter. Likewise, communities want a quality school curriculum in which children learn spoken and unspoken positive behaviors. They expect school employees to strengthen academic content (the planned curriculum) and reinforce prosocial behavior (the unplanned curriculum). Together, schools, parents, and communities can develop a top-notch curriculum, one that recognizes student achievement and encourages peaceful conduct.

Multicultural Peace

Schools have become culturally diverse with children representing various ethnic, cultural, and racial groups. In some school districts, there is a sense of urgency to renew curriculum content or replace it with multicultural content. They face the challenge of aligning materials with the experiences of youngsters who do not fit homogeneous middle-class or upper-class norms. The faculty and staff are learning to teach multicultural education and ways to help reduce the social and cultural gaps that exist between school and home.

Table 4.3 The Complete Performance Review: A Self-Directed Analysis of Multicultural Teaching

1. Classroom climate	List efforts to create a positive learning environment for students to feel at ease in class regardless of gender, race, language, culture, or disability.
2. Creative curricula	List efforts to supplement the standard curricula with culturally diverse information, activities, and materials.
3. Complimentary communication	List efforts to use both oral and written statements to show respect for the ethnic identity of students.
4. Planned progress	Identify methods employed to assess the ongoing progress of student learning as well as methods to prevent students from blaming or using their ethnicity as an excuse for underachieving.
5. Particular practices	Identify monocultural teaching practices and skills that have been replaced with multicultural practices.
6. Productive performance	Identify the multicultural factors that interfere with teaching performance or restrict productivity.
7. Reflective teaching	Describe approaches for thinking reflectively about unfair situations or inequalities that result from making certain teaching decisions.
8. Reliable tools	Describe the teaching tools relied on most in helping students understand and accept the cultural diversity of others, such as electronic devices, audiovisual aids, print media, and photographs.
9. Relevant training	Describe involvement in professional development or training activities to enhance knowledge about multicultural education.

SOURCE: Adapted from Bey (1986).

Successfully implanted multicultural content in a supportive school climate promotes diversity and nurtures multicultural peace among students. This kind of peace encourages cultural groups to cooperate and communicate, to value ethnic diversity, and to care about each other. Overall, the faculty and staff recognize multiculturalism by teaching students to tolerate, appreciate, and understand the differences and similarities among people.

In working with children from diverse cultural backgrounds, school personnel may benefit from a multicultural analysis. The self-directed analysis of multicultural teaching (Table 4.3) is designed for educators to conduct a comprehensive performance review. It identifies nine categories for an individual to determine how he or she teaches to reach a diverse group of learners.

Fundamentally, multicultural peace advocates a change in the violent behavior of individuals who hurt, harm, or destroy the belongings of others because of cultural or racial hatred. It encourages them to solve cultural hostilities nonviolently and study the peacemaking practices of different ethnic groups.

Multicultural Curricular Approaches

Curricular approaches delineated specifically for multicultural education offer strategies to consider when reforming the curriculum. The five multicultural approaches identified by Sleeter and Grant (1988) are suggested to help plan for multicultural peace. In describing each curricular approach, the brackets indicate information added to emphasize peace.

The Exceptional and Culturally Different Approach. This includes curriculum plans that are organized around strategies to help students of color, low-income households, special education needs, or a combination of these to achieve, assimilate, [and survive in a violent society].

The Human Relations Approach. This includes curriculum activities that are organized to help students foster positive interpersonal relationships, strengthen their self-concept, [and develop social skills to improve their interaction among members of diverse groups].

The Single-Group Studies Approach. This approach includes curriculum plans that are organized as separate lessons or subject units to help raise the students' consciousness about a group by teaching its history, culture, and contributions, [as well as factors that account for the harmony and disharmony among members of the group].

The Multicultural Approach. This includes rewriting curriculum plans to reflect diversity and uphold equality throughout the entire educational process. All aspects of teaching and learning are transformed to promote [peace and] equal academic achievement across groups. The transformation will reduce or eliminate the practice of tracking and ability grouping to differentiate pupil achievement and learning.

The Multicultural and Social Reconstructionist Approach. This includes combining the curriculum plans of single-group studies with the multicultural approach. Students learn to analyze the inequality and oppression in our society, examine social problems [related to juvenile delinquency], and create ways to effect social change.

These curricular approaches provide a range of ideas to consider when planning, developing, or renewing multicultural content to include peace. Regardless of what approach is implemented, there exists an opportunity for faculty to become more knowledgeable about the ethnic and racial groups that characterize the people of the United States and the world.

Last, multicultural education can combat real problems when it addresses the social consequences of gang, physical, and racial violence. It must go beyond the simple transfer of skills to adjustments in attitude and behavior to empower students to lead productive lives (Nieto, 1992).

Multicultural Content

There are many different ways to organize and use multicultural content. The content can be multidisciplinary covering various grade levels and subject areas. Five categories of use outlined by Banks (1992) identify ways in which multicultural content can be applied.

Empowerment. All members of the faculty and staff participate in examining and restructuring the culture and organization of the school. They are empowered to promote gender, racial, and social class equality within the school culture and social structure.

Equity Pedagogy. Teachers modify multicultural content and instruction to facilitate the academic achievement of students. They also vary methods of teaching according to the wide range of learning styles within various cultural and ethnic groups.

Prejudice Reduction. Teaching materials and learning activities include images of ethnic and racial groups to help students develop more positive racial attitudes.

Knowledge Construction. The teacher becomes involved in helping students understand the different cultural assumptions, perspectives, and biases in the ways knowledge bases are constructed (e.g., Columbus's arrival in the Caribbean from two perspectives, the sailors' and the Arawak Indians').

Content Integration. The teacher integrates the subject with multicultural content to illustrate key concepts, principles, generalizations, and theories from several ethnic groups.

Infusing various dimensions of multicultural concepts and practices throughout the school serves several purposes. First, the content has an effect on the way teachers prepare their lessons. Second, the content reinforces the learning of specific academic skills. Finally, the content benefits a diverse student population witnessing the occurrence of social conflicts in our society.

Social Peace

Appeals to stop violence and reinstate social peace have been heard in virtually every community throughout the nation. In responding to the appeals, schools have to refine their role in teaching social peace. The cultivation of social peace includes teaching children and youth nonviolent cooperation, participation, and communication. A curriculum that fails to interfuse the social maturity and competence of students may leave them with limited social interaction skills.

The design of curriculum plans can no longer exclude information that will prepare students to combat school violence by caring for each other. One means of encouraging primary and upper elementary children to care for themselves and others is through a social curriculum. Such a curriculum helps them gain social skills (Charney, 1991) and builds peaceful relations in the classroom (see the Appendix, Resource A: Social Peace Curriculum for Primary and Elementary Schools).

Also, the curriculum for middle and high school students has to include specific information for their age groups. It must focus on the concerns teenagers have about physical growth and development, peer acceptance and rejection, personal friendships and dating, social status, and progress in school. In addition, the curriculum should emphasize personal safety and help them cope with the following worries.

- Fear of victimization by hostile schoolmates, bullies, and gang members
- Apprehension about interpersonal conflict, violence, sex, and illicit drugs
- Force of peer pressure to participate in violent crime

Teenagers have to manage these fears, assume responsibility for their own actions, set constructive goals to direct their lives, and build their confidence. Teachers, counselors, administrators, and parents can foster this confidence by listening and talking to students about things that hinder their success. Aspects of the social peace curriculum should emphasize human qualities such as perseverance, persistence, and patience.

The qualities and values that enable adults to prevail in challenging circumstances are the ones teenagers need to know to plan safe solutions to problems. Knowing how to plan, solve problems, and make choices can enhance the academic and personal success of students. A secondary level social curriculum (see the Appendix, Resource B) has to include opportunities for them to learn the precautions necessary to protect their lives as peaceful and productive citizens.

Planning for Change

In organizing a group to develop or modify curricula, there is no one procedure or design that will suffice for all schools. Here are some possible projects for a group to consider:

- Examine the present curriculum materials for all grade levels to identify areas where concepts, skills, and practices related to social peace or multicultural peace need improvement (see Table 4.4).
- Poll teachers, students, and parents to determine their curricular preferences. Report the survey findings in the community newspaper as well as the curriculum areas targeted for change.

Table 4.4 Surveying Curriculum Materials

Review your school's curriculum and materials to determine if the following topics, issues, and problems are included.

Yes	No	
___	___	1. Social values are addressed as well as principles and values of a democratic society.
___	___	2. Global concerns and problems are included.
___	___	3. Cultural, ethnic, and racial factors relevant to building social unity among groups are addressed.
___	___	4. Human rights and civil rights are acknowledged.
___	___	5. Social challenges related to freedom, justice, and dignity are addressed.
___	___	6. National unity and identity emphasizing the common good across ethnic groups are acknowledged.
___	___	7. People from all cultures who have worked as peacemakers and contributed to society are prominently featured in up-to-date materials.
___	___	8. Conflict resolution, mediation skills, effective communication, personal responsibility, multiculturalism, and tolerance are taught with every subject.

- Develop a rationale for the proposed curriculum and a time-table outlining the completion of activities. The documentation of events leading to the finished curriculum may include an action research project for individuals interested in studying the process of curriculum change.

Regardless of what curriculum planning process is applied, both teacher ownership and administrative support are needed. The planning shall require preparation of teachers to implement the curriculum content and activities effectively. They should also be encouraged to extend and personalize teaching approaches by developing their own supplementary materials. Efforts to make peace a reality can start with conceptions of peaceable ideas for teachers to transmit in class. Mastering their ability to interfuse peacemaking skills and subject matter will add new dimensions to curriculum reform.

Closing Thoughts

Schools for peace across the curricula in favor of planning must realize that their induction of children into the American culture is happening at a time when society is faced with the pressures of violence. So, in educating pupils for real-life situations, curriculum planners may agree with Hass (1987). He defends the need to consider the "social forces as reflected in (1) social goals, (2) cultural uniformity and diversity, (3) social pressures, (4) social change, (5) future planning, and (6) concepts of culture" (p. 7).

Let's Talk

1. What approaches might you use to develop curriculum related to social peace?
2. What approaches might you use to develop curriculum related to multicultural peace?
3. What social and ethical issues would you like to see included across the curriculum?
4. What human qualities and values make the hidden curriculum unpredictable?
5. What type of resources should the school library maintain on local, national, and international peacemakers?

Suggested Activities

1. Invite curriculum specialists to meet with teachers to describe ways to interfuse social peace and subject area knowledge.
2. Arrange a meeting for teachers to brainstorm ideas to plan, develop, and implement peace across the curriculum.
3. Organize a "Show and Tell" program for skilled teachers to demonstrate the use of multicultural materials.
4. Conduct a survey to determine the level of assistance faculty and staff need to manage the hidden curriculum effectively.
5. Contact organizations to obtain the resources needed to develop social peace materials and activities (see the Appendix, Resource B).
6. Write a newsletter article encouraging teachers to emphasize peacemaking skills in their lessons.

PRINCIPLE 5

The methods of instruction should maximize the students' learning potential and empower them to solve problems peacefully.

ᏍᎧ 5 ᏍᎧ

Changing Instruction

The Hard Realities

To bring about instructional reform, teachers' potential to be thoughtful and deliberate architects of teaching and learning in their own classrooms must be tapped and supported.
Cochran-Smith and Lytle (1993, p. 101)

One of the hard realities is the teachers' ability to govern the instructional process for students to excel academically. Motivating pupils to learn and practice peace is a challenge to the autonomy teachers have in selecting teaching styles, instructional activities, supplementary resources, and curriculum materials. Some teachers exert classroom control, overlooking opportunities for pupils to have alternate lessons and instructional methods presented on a regular basis. They set the tone for a peaceable atmosphere as well as the expectations for student success. With the authority to govern classrooms, teachers exhibit different teaching styles—*authoritarian, democratic,* and *laissez-faire* (Moore, 1989).

The authoritarian approach uses pressure, criticism, and punishment. In such a classroom, students feel uneasy and fear the teacher's authority. In the democratic approach, the teacher is considerate, caring, and warm, but also firm when students disobey; the classroom is friendly, and students do not encounter put-downs or criticism when they make mistakes. In the laissez-faire approach, the teacher allows students to have freedom with limits and provides them with the guidance to become responsible learners.

We know that just as teachers' control varies, so does the control students have in determining how much and how long to be active in the learning process. In thinking about the instructional compatibility between students and teachers at your school, consider the following question.

What style of teacher authority is needed for students to learn peacefully?

Differentiated Instruction

The lockstep method—teaching the whole class with one approach without preparing learning activities to meet the diverse capabilities of students—should not be standard practice. Instead, approaches to stimulate the interests of both high and low achievers should be continually developed in every classroom. Teachers can differentiate instruction using some of the following approaches (Association for Supervision and Curriculum Development, 1994).

Mastery Learning. Curriculum units and lessons are organized for students to learn at different rates. If a student fails to grasp key concepts and skills from a unit, he or she receives additional instruction from the teacher while others in the class move on to supplementary activities.

Learning Centers. Work stations are located in different sections of the classroom, and students are able to rotate among various stations designed to help them meet specific learning objectives. Students work at their own pace, and the teacher moves about the room to facilitate and keep students on task.

Cooperative Learning. The learning objectives for students are interdependent as they work together to accomplish shared goals. Students are divided into small groups and help each other complete assigned activities and tasks. The teacher may group and regroup students according to individual progress, interest, and work style.

Contracts. Work contracts describe the learning objectives and activities students will perform each day until the contract expires. The contracts are usually formal agreements between teacher and student, but sometime a parent will be invited to sign the contract. On a contractual basis, students learn on their own and accomplish goals unrelated to those of other classmates.

Direct Instruction. The teacher explains in systematic steps what students are expected to learn, helping them understand the purpose and result of each step. In using direct instruction, the teacher gives clear directions leading students through a process (e.g., study skills, test-taking skills) and teaches them to use the process as a skill to master other academic skills.

Self-Directed Projects. Students may choose individual or group projects on topics that interest them. They produce a product that can be used by others (e.g., video, computer software, handbook).

Service Learning. Community service assignments are integrated into the curriculum for students to participate in activities that serve people. They gain firsthand knowledge of what it is like to help others in hospitals, nursing homes, or day-care centers.

Electronic Learning. This type of instruction involves the use of electronic tools and devices to educate. Knowledge is dispensed via computer-based learning, cassette and videotape playback, educational television, and distance learning communications in which cameras, monitors, microphones, facsimiles, and telephones enable teachers and students in different locations to share resources.

These differentiated approaches allow for greater learner participation in the instructional process. They offer several "comfort zones" for students to absorb and retain new content. Otherwise, teachers may unknowingly frustrate a student, as shown in the following story (George, Stevenson, Thomason, & Beane, 1992).

Sitting at the back of the room, an observer watched as a group of 8th-graders worked through the lengthy test that their teacher gave at the end of each unit. Having glanced furtively backward several times, one of the students finally turned to the observer and said, "This test is stupid."

The observer, supposing this was just another one of those notorious 8th-grade behaviors, said nothing.

"This is stupid," the student protested again, this time in a louder voice.

Not wanting to create a scene, the observer whispered, "What's stupid?"

"This," said the student, pushing the test forward.

It was a test like other tests, several pages filled with multiple-choice, matching, and short-answer questions. So the observer said, "It doesn't look stupid. It just looks like the teacher is trying to find out whether you learned what you were supposed to."

"That's what's stupid about it. It's all what the teacher thinks we should know. Why don't they ever want to know what *we* know." (p. 81)

The student certainly conveys a message to be heeded by those in classrooms where learning is assessed and filtered primarily through tests. Busy classrooms do not allow much time for teachers to reflect or reevaluate instructional decisions. The disturbing claim that they show little concern about what students actually know may be justified. One may wonder whether certain instructional approaches remain unchanged because teachers neither have the time nor the preparation to implement new methods.

Multiple Intelligences

An advancement in student achievement is possible when diverse intellectual functions are recognized. Research conducted by Gardner (1983) indicates that children have differing patterns of strengths and weaknesses in seven intelligence domains, which include the following patterns of intellectual functioning (Armstrong, 1994; Gardner & Hatch, 1989).

Linguistic Intelligence. This is the ability to use language to excite, please, convince, stimulate, or convey information. Students have the capacity to use words effectively, either orally or in writing.

Logical-Mathematical Intelligence. This is the ability to explore patterns, categories, and relationships by manipulating objects or symbols and to experiment in a controlled, orderly way. Students have the capacity to use numbers effectively and to reason well.

Spatial Intelligence. This is the ability to perceive and mentally manipulate a form or object to create tension, balance, and composition in a visual or spatial display. Students have the ability to perceive the visual-spatial world accurately and to transform visual perceptions.

Musical Intelligence. This is the ability to enjoy, perform, or compose a musical piece. Students have the capacity to perceive, discriminate, transform, and express themselves through music.

Bodily-Kinesthetic Intelligence. This is the ability to use fine and gross motor skills in sports, the performing arts, or arts and crafts production. Students have expertise in using the whole body to express ideas and feelings.

Intrapersonal Intelligence. This is the ability to gain access to and understand one's inner feelings, dreams, and ideas. Students possess self-knowledge and can adapt their actions accordingly.

Interpersonal Intelligence. This is the ability to understand and get along with others. Students possess the ability to perceive and make distinctions in the moods, intentions, motivations, and feelings of other people.

Each intellectual pattern has implications for structuring the curriculum to engage multiple intelligences. Students will benefit when the teacher gives equal time to each domain (Armstrong, 1994). When students have strengths in some domains and not in others, the teacher can provide help to build their skills in the weak areas.

Understanding the Student

A reality for today's child is being a member of a generation learning to depend on computerized energy. Although education moves slowly, the world outside the classroom is moving very fast with the help of technology. In an effort to understand particular needs, a person can start by asking what the primary, upper elementary, middle school, and high school students are like.

Primary Level

Young children possess the unspoiled desire to learn how to do things and to please others, especially their parents. Their excitement and eagerness convey an optimistic outlook on life. This optimism can turn to pessimism if frightening experiences cause certain apprehensions. For example, it is normal for children to resist going outside to play when they live in neighborhoods where drive-by shootings or gang fights occur. Their natural curiosity about life seems to fade as they are reminded constantly by teachers and parents, "Do not take candy or money from strangers," "Do not get in the car with a stranger," and "Do not walk home from school alone."

The guidance children receive to protect them from harm is necessary because they are socially, physically, and emotionally immature. Their involvement in destructive violence is minimal, particularly when adults supervise them closely. They require careful supervision while forming a self-image of who they are as individuals. Until they learn or are told differently, children have a sincere willingness to help and tend to trust adults. Although life experiences can be limited, the youngsters' development of skepticism and favoritism is part of the process of growing up.

Upper Elementary Level

"How does an airplane stay in the air?" "Why can't we swim under water like fish?" These are the questions of upper elementary children exploring their world and probing for answers. Freedom of exploration allows them to discover new things. In this discovery process, they sometimes want adults to do more than provide simple answers to questions.

Developing the normal ability to handle complex ideas, they understand what education is about and tend to like school. This may not be the case, however, for children who receive a great deal of criticism. When they are told, "You can never get things right," "You're so dumb," or "You don't listen," these statements attack their self-esteem. If disgraced and embarrassed at school, they can lose interest in the learning process and start to dislike school.

Also, children living in households where family problems hinder their ability to learn and study may not find school as exciting as children in households where education is a top priority. If they live in temporary facilities for the homeless, family shelters, or foster homes, negative feelings can arise from having to do without the valuable belongings that other children bring or wear to school. Some of them may be inclined to steal, making them vulnerable to crime.

One way to reach elementary students headed for trouble is through instruction that motivates them to learn. If they find school interesting and take learning seriously, it is possible for them to stay away from criminal elements in the community. Although most children like to be with youngsters their own age, teachers and parents should occasionally ask if they are being picked on by bullies or if friends are forcing them to commit violent acts.

Middle School Level

"I just got my ears pierced; let's do yours." In this statement, the student is being urged to join in by having his or her ears pierced. Peer pressure is hard to resist when youths want to behave like their friends in school. Accepting advice from peers to look like everyone else is common in middle-junior high school. Also, talking to friends about personal concerns, either at school or at home by telephone, is a major part of their world.

It is not uncommon for adolescents to find themselves doing or saying things they once considered indecent behavior. For example, smoking, using drugs, drinking alcohol, and having sex are some of the behaviors they reconsider at middle school level. If adults fail to provide guidance concerning these behaviors, the information they receive from peers may be misleading or false.

Disruptive middle schoolers will act on dares; they'll break school rules without stopping to think how the consequences of their actions might harm or hurt others. Presenting them with information about crime, illegal acts, and juvenile offenses is not always enough to curtail violent, risk-taking behavior. At times, they may make poor decisions because of their loyalty to peers. Their difficulty in defining what is right and wrong points out the need for them to talk with teachers, counselors, or parents about their problems.

Teachers cannot expect all adolescents to know how to handle physical growth and development. In some situations, middle-junior high students begin to look older than their actual age, and high school teenagers may be interested in dating them. This is a stage of life in which boys and girls may not like talking with adults about the physical changes they are experiencing.

High School Level

High school is hard work for those students who compete for good grades, honors, and recognition. Those who are not in the competitive academic mode may also work hard, facing the real world of part-time employment, car insurance, or caring for their baby as a teenage parent. In planning for the future, teenagers want information for use in adulthood. They also need outlets to help them relieve stress (e.g., sports activities, dances, plays).

As for ethics and values, teenagers set their own in making choices for themselves. They also make problem-solving decisions but seem to dislike being held accountable for the consequences of bad decisions. Managing the pressure of refusing enticements by friends who use the excuse, "If I got away with it, so can you," is difficult. As a result, violent teenagers contribute to our societal ills. They kill, stab, mug, rape, and abuse other people, sometimes for no reason other than to satisfy an urge to commit a destructive criminal act.

Antiviolence messages containing factual and statistical information showing the dangers and consequences of violating local, state, and federal laws must be reinforced in the classroom. Teachers who are afraid to confront or have disputes with hostile teenagers may feel uneasy about enforcing school rules. Nevertheless, the stressors in the lives of disruptive students overshadow the instructional process as they suppress education unrelated to dealing with the hard realities of our society.

Table 5.1 Preventing Violence-Related Conflicts

---

1. When angry, separate yourself from the situation and take the time to calm down.
2. Attack the problem, not the person or persons involved.
3. Communicate your feelings clearly and assertively.
4. Focus on the issue, not on your position about the issue.
5. Accept and respect opinions that may differ, try not to force compliance, and work to reach a common agreement.
6. Do not view the situation as a competition where one has to win and one has to lose. Work toward solutions for both persons to have some of their needs met.
7. Focus on areas of common agreement and interest, rather than areas of disagreement and opposition.
8. Never jump to conclusions or make assumptions about what the other person is thinking or feeling.
9. Listen without interrupting, and ask for more information and feedback, if needed, to ensure a clear understanding of the issue.
10. Remember, if only one person's needs are satisfied, then the conflict has not been resolved and may continue.

SOURCE: Adapted from Costen (1994).

Conflicts

Students unaware of ways to solve disputes will find conflict prevention strategies helpful in getting along with others. They learn to understand themselves as individuals, analyze situations, communicate their desires, and respond to different and conflicting views. Placing an emphasis on the proactive skills used to solve disputes is an instructional obligation. Certainly, as one would expect, "teachers can do a great deal to challenge the violence in children's lives; they can intervene early and teach specific skills that will help children learn a broader repertoire for resolving their conflicts" (Carlsson-Paige & Levin, 1992, p. 8).

Students may or may not understand that when basic needs such as freedom and belonging are not met, disputes can occur; also, conflicts can occur when resources are limited or values differ. The strategies in Table 5.1 will help them manage friction.

Furthermore, situations like the one in the following scenario may take place during the school day.

The lunch period is 40 minutes at Short Tail School. Gerald and his best friend Ken have been waiting in a long, slow line to purchase their lunch. They have only 20 minutes left until the bell rings. Roger, a student in their class, rushes in front of them, jumps the line, and tells everyone he has to eat in a hurry because he is just starving and will not be able to eat again until late that night. Roger goes on to say he has to take a make-up test in 15 minutes, has band practice until 6:00 p.m. that evening, and then has to find someone to help him complete a science project that is due tomorrow. Ken shoves Roger out of line and insists that he wait his turn. Roger and Ken glare at each other and exchange insults. Gerald stands there, not sure what to do.

Proactive conflict prevention would encourage these students to settle their disagreement without shoving each other. They needed to know how to be creative and in control of reaching an agreement without hurting each other.

Problem-Solving Skills

The development of students' problem-solving skills starts with the application of an approach for making decisions. They should have an approach designed to guide their thinking. An eight-step method for solving stressful social dilemmas as well as academic work (e.g., math, science) can help them handle a full range of situations. A teacher, parent, or counselor would have students apply the following steps developed by Elias and Clabby (1992):

1. *Look for signs of different feelings.* Recognize the early idiosyncratic signs of your own feelings and stress as well as those of others.
2. *Tell yourself what the problem is.* Be able to describe your upset in specific, behavioral terms.
3. *Decide on your goal.* Determine specifically what you want to have happen.
4. *Stop and think of as many solutions to the problem as you can.* Brainstorm solutions that relate to the goal.
5. *For each solution, think of all the things that might happen next.* Anticipate consequences.
6. *Choose your best solution.* Make a selection from among some well-considered options.

7. *Plan it and make a final check.* Mentally rehearse when, where, and how a best solution will be implemented as well as anticipating and dealing with potential obstacles.

8. *Try it and rethink it.* Implement the planned solution and review the outcome. (pp. 171-172)

Practicing this eight-step approach is a slow process at first, but gradually, with the teacher's help, students get to know the steps. After extended use, the strategy becomes personally meaningful and useful, and students will collapse the steps to suit their needs.

In order to be specific about details, here is a problem-solving technique that uses an action plan. When there is formal planning as a part of problem solving, it engages students in the process of documenting their intentions. The following steps will encourage them to analyze what is needed or expected to address their problem.

1. Identify the problem. Defining the problem allows students to work with the problem, not a symptom.

2. Decide on the causes and possible solutions. Separating the causes and issues involved in the problem helps isolate the area of concern and zero in on the core issue.

3. Develop a plan of action. Evaluating a course of action allows students to engage in critical thinking, decision making, and selecting strategies to address the issue.

4. Implement the plan of action. Responding to an issue when a course of action has been designated allows the student to organize, consider varying possibilities, and do something about the issue.

5. Reflect on the plan. Analyzing its effectiveness provides a critique of the strengths and weaknesses of the plan.

6. Change the approach. If the initial course of action is not successful, try a new approach.

This six-step procedure can be modeled in any class to show students how to prevent problems from escalating. This procedure could be beneficial in their learning peacemaking and decision-making skills.

Lastly, voluntary problem solving between two individuals trying to reach a joint agreement is considered *negotiation* (Messing, 1993).

Learning negotiation skills to reach agreement in a peaceable manner includes certain procedures. For example, the following behaviors outlined by Drew (1987) refer to a series of *conflict resolution* actions two individuals can perform to resolve problems.

1. When upset, each person finds alternate ways to express anger.
2. Using "I" messages, each person states his or her feelings about the problem without interruption, blaming, or name calling.
3. Each person states the problem as the other person sees it.
4. Each person states how he or she is responsible for the problem.
5. Together, both people brainstorm solutions and choose one that satisfies them both.
6. Each person affirms the other partner.

Closing Thoughts

Proactive strategies, such as differentiated instructional approaches, add to the alternatives educators and students need to institute problem-solving and peacemaking activities, thus reducing inappropriate behaviors (Houston & Grubaugh, 1989). Opportunities to change negative behavior and adjust to new learning experiences may cause all parties to openly articulate interests, ideas, and questions. Be willing to examine efforts to address the hard realities of teaching from a variety of perspectives, and listen to the views of peacemakers.

Let's Talk

1. In your opinion, what kinds of instructional changes are needed at your school?
2. Why should parents, teachers, and administrators be interested in multiple intelligences?
3. Tell what happened the last time you applied problem-solving skills to avoid or solve a conflict.

4. Describe the ways in which you get to know and understand students.

5. What kinds of problems would you like students to solve on their own?

Suggested Activities

1. Prepare a handout sheet for faculty and staff with suggestions about differential instructional approaches.

2. Conduct an inservice program for teachers and parents on multiple intelligences (refer to Armstrong, 1994).

3. Prepare a list of activities to help school employees take time to stop, think, wonder, explore, and analyze their work in relation to understanding children and youth.

4. Develop demonstration lessons for teachers and students to learn social problem-solving techniques, peer mediation strategies, and conflict resolution skills (see the Appendix, Resource H).

5. Organize faculty members in small groups to discuss the pros and cons of various instructional methods (see pp. 70-71) to help students master their academic work. Ask them to give examples of how they present certain methods. The groups can use a problem-solving approach as they talk about their instructional concerns. For example, they could (a) define the problems, (b) define the causes, and (c) prepare plans for change. At the end of this activity, ask group members what they liked most and least about the problem-solving method. Also ask them what they would change, and why.

PRINCIPLE 6

The parents should support the learning experiences of children and facilitate the school's effort to teach social values.

❧ 6 ❧

Working With Parents

*Tight-knit social networks of approving and disapproving
people are more effective determinants of a child's behavior
than laws, policemen, security, and surveillance equipment.
Eventually, the attitudes, values, and behavior of the adult
authority figures become a part of a child's character.*

Comer (1980, p. 10)

Children need approving authority figures: teachers and parents
who will respect and listen to them. They may want to talk with
adults but are sometimes reluctant to do so, fearing that no one will
understand or care. In some households, children compete for their
parents' time and attention, particularly if the parents are seldom
home. Adults have to realize that children are thinkers who can
communicate and discuss their ideas if someone is there to listen.

Parent-Child Communication

Communication between parent and child is a basis of support,
information, and a less stressful way to manage potential problems
associated with growing up. The school can implement activities for
parents to learn to communicate effectively with their children. In

working with parents to develop the appropriate communication skills, the bottom line is to increase student motivation, achievement, and success in school. An additional emphasis would be for parents to interact more with their children at home to instill the value of education.

It is essential, too, for adults to understand different communication techniques and ways of responding to children in conversation. A few of the techniques include listening, observing, and responding (U.S. Department of Education, 1990). In each of these areas, there are key behaviors for both parents and teachers to consider.

1. *Listen*

   Pay attention.

   Don't interrupt.

   Don't prepare what you will say while the child is speaking.

   Reserve judgment until the child has finished and has asked you for a response.

2. *Observe*

   Be aware of the child's facial expression and body language. Is the child nervous or uncomfortable—frowning, drumming fingers, tapping a foot, looking at the clock? Or does the child seem relaxed—smiling, looking you in the eyes? Reading these signs will help parents and teachers know how the child is feeling.

   During the conversation, acknowledge what the child is saying —move your body forward if you are sitting, touch a shoulder if you are walking, or nod your head and make eye contact.

3. *Respond*

   Consider the following statements: "I am very concerned about . . . " and "I understand that it is sometimes difficult . . . " are better ways to respond to the child than beginning sentences with, "You should," "If I were you," or "When I was your age, we didn't . . . " Speaking for oneself sounds thoughtful and is less likely to be considered a lecture or an automatic response.

   If the child tells you something you don't want to hear, don't ignore the statement.

> Don't offer advice in response to every statement the child makes. It is better to listen carefully to what is being said and try to understand the real feelings behind the words.
>
> Make sure you understand what the child means. Repeat things to the child for confirmation.

When healthy communication occurs, students seek advice or ask for the help of an adult. Further, parents and teachers should take time to listen and try to see the world through the child's eyes. Remember, problems easy for adults to solve can be overwhelming for children.

School and Family

In communities where parents are involved in their children's education, students achieve more than children whose parents do not become involved in school activities (Baker & Stevenson, 1986; Useem, 1990). Realizing the importance of parent involvement in student success, schools have to make an effort for parents to become and stay involved in their children's education.

School and family share a major responsibility because both of them influence the educational success and failure of their children. For example, when students fail, "some blame the child and the family for their weaknesses and deficiencies. Interestingly, if students succeed, schools and families both claim responsibility, and sometimes even acknowledge each other's contribution to 'children's success'" (Epstein, 1992). Agreeing to share the contributions represents a functioning partnership; however, this may not be the case in communities where obstacles lie between the school and the family.

Maintaining workable partnerships to increase or improve parental participation in school activities involves the removal of certain obstacles. One in particular is the situation where teachers contact the parent only when the child is experiencing learning or behavioral problems in school. Another barrier is the practice of some parents, who do not contact the school unless their child is experiencing or showing signs of unusual distress at home.

Schools without significant parental involvement should look critically at their practices to stay in contact with the home. In some communities, the schools may inadvertently create limitations

(Hamilton & Osborne, 1994) that bring about the following barriers: (a) physical, (b) social, (c) emotional, and (d) communication. Physical barriers relate to the frustrations parents have in making arrangements to attend school events. For some parents, the problems might be finding a babysitter, having inappropriate transportation, or being unable to take time away from work.

In terms of social barriers, the limitations have to do with family values regarding education. Also, there are households in which personal and social problems prevent parent involvement (e.g., drug dependency, alcoholism, mental illness, homelessness). As for emotional barriers, it is difficult to erase the unpleasant memories of parents who had negative experiences or social rejection when they attended school. In addition, they may be reluctant to voice concerns about the school or the teacher, not wanting to cause problems for their children.

Last, communication barriers relate to the methods used to keep parents informed and the welcome they receive when attending school functions. If parents do not read or speak English, then written and verbal communications should be in their native language.

School and family partnerships can thrive if these barriers are addressed from the perspective of understanding the choices that parents make concerning their ability to support school activities. The level at which parents may or may not participate does not affect their primary interest in the safety of their children at school.

Family Education

Family education is promoted through schools that include parents in the educational process. In working with parents as partners in learning, family education programs are effective when they encourage both teachers and parents to do the following:

- Take advantage of the school support systems when a child is having learning difficulties
- Find time and ways to nurture the child's learning at home
- Be responsible partners in guiding the child's learning and development
- Observe the classroom to monitor the child's progress
- Agree on family rules for helping the child complete school assignments

Family education has to involve members of the household in the educational process. In order to help everyone become more involved, school personnel can make home visits to talk to parents and explain information on child development and learning. These visits will benefit the parents of preschoolers who need information on early learning and school requirements for the primary grades. Also, schools and public libraries may have a section available for parents to borrow books on parenthood and books to read aloud to their children. Activities such as these will build a positive link between families and school.

Parent Workshops

As mentors of children, it is imperative for parents and teachers to support positive, peaceful student behavior. If possible, schools should conduct workshops for parents. Here are a few of the topics the workshops might address:

- *Personal safety*—Increasing security precautions
- *Discipline*—Setting rules and consequences and enforcing them
- *Time management*—Planning study time, playtime, and an appropriate bedtime
- *Communication skills*—Engaging in give-and-take conversations with children about learning
- *Homework*—Providing a quiet place to do schoolwork, and knowing the quality of work expected by the teacher
- *Self-esteem*—Building parents' confidence in guiding their children
- *Drug and alcohol abuse*—Learning about the dangers of drug and alcohol use and what to do about it
- *Nutrition*—Planning and cooking wholesome meals for the family

Workshops containing helpful, productive, and idea-oriented information will fulfill the interest of parents. Participants gain the personal satisfaction of knowing they can have direct involvement in learning how to make a substantial difference in the lives of children—acting on the notion that they can progress in learning to become better parents. Such participation corroborates the belief that schools should establish stronger contacts with parents and concerned citizens.

Adult Supervision

Regularly, schools and social agencies remind parents not to leave young children unsupervised at home. As for unsupervised teenagers, they are more likely to become involved in violence or other delinquent behavior. Lack of adult supervision and guidance can lead to a host of unwarranted problems (e.g., pregnancy, theft, alcohol, drug use). A few short statements from problem teenagers point out some of the difficulties.

Candie: I would play hooky from school. Just hang out with my girlfriend, or maybe my boyfriend, or my house when my mom left for work.

Globe: I watch my sister go from job to job when she dropped out of school and she never had any money. The money thing ain't working out. I won't drop out.

Genie: I decided to keep my baby. I take one step at a time and just work it out that way.

Horse: If I didn't stop drugs, I thought, I'm going to die. I'd go to school, and by fourth period, I'd fall asleep. I was sick.

Peaches: I had a bad problem. I didn't like myself and I didn't want to live.

These students need parental guidance and help with their social lives and failing academic progress. The limited time and attention given to education caused them to behave and perform poorly in school. Certainly the amount of time students devote to studying is strongly related to academic performance. Effective use of time away from school to reinforce what is learned in the classroom helps student progress. Unfortunately, those who need to spend more time at home on academic activities may find other things to do if parents are not at home.

Hopefully, some of the supervisory measures suggested by educators will help parents maintain control and know where their children are at all times. Some actions parents can take include these:

- Asking children to talk about school and to show their school-work and homework

- Enforcing community curfews and restricting activities during the school week

- Asking children if the school gave them notes, letters, or reports for the parents to sign

- Questioning children about any disputes or conflicts they may have encountered with other classmates

- Talking to children about their experiences to help them identify and extract meaning from events, movies, and stories

- Restricting time to watch television, and limiting time spent talking on the telephone

- Encouraging use of the school and public library, and requiring children to spend a certain amount of time reading each day

- Making school activities a top priority, and preparing a study area in the house where children feel comfortable doing homework

Instill Values

Family structure and lifestyle influence the habits, ideas, and attitudes that children develop. In establishing a peaceful learning environment, teachers and administrators must be sensitive to situations in which family values conflict with school values. As Rich (1993) has noted:

We know that . . . public schools emphasize such middle-class values as achievement, hard work, competition, cleanliness, respect for authority, negotiation, orderliness, and self-control over impulses. Above all, they place emphasis on the belief that people who apply themselves get ahead in school and in life. Seldom mentioned are those who rely on family connections, wealth, power, and influence to advance or maintain an important position or high status. The prevailing value is on personal achievement—to achieve, one must compete but compete fairly. This is evident in the sorting and screening mechanisms used in the school system: grades, tests, honors, and scholarships. Differences are to be settled by discussion, negotiation, and compromise rather than coercion or violence. Students are expected to control their impulses in order to build character and help maintain an orderly school environment. Children who have not had these school values instilled and reinforced in the home are at a disadvantage. (p. 164)

In the practices and customs at home, parental values may conflict with school policies and state laws. For example, in states where corporal punishment is legal, the chastisement inflicted on the body of a child can be a form of punishment opposed by parents for moral, religious, or other reasons. Such punishment is not conducive to a peaceful school climate and does not model an acceptable way to correct misconduct. School districts may emphasize social responsibility, character education, or social problem-solving skills to deal with disruptive student conduct (Richardson & Evans, 1993).

The comments adults express about education, as well as factors related to the parents' education, income, and outlook on life, can affect the academic achievement of children. Values learned inside and outside the home are affected by the way parents manage and regulate their child's participation in community activities and peer relationships (Parke & Ladd, 1992).

One value typically instilled during childhood is the expectation parents hold for their children to secure a college education and be successful in the professional world. College-bound students in affluent neighborhoods are likely to say that their parents have plans for them to attend college. In low-socioeconomic households, parents with aspirations for their children to attend college must reinforce the expectation by talking to them about the importance of a good education.

Success in school requires hard work and study. In motivating children to learn, teachers and parents should do the following:

- Emphasize the importance of qualities such as honesty, courage, and loyalty.
- Use a peaceful manner in explaining to children the ideals underlying positive and negative decisions.
- Point out the consequences of mistakes or failures in living up to promises.

- Share personal experiences and stories to reinforce the message that effort, persistence, and a good reputation count.
- Talk about the achievements of prominent leaders who rose from humble beginnings and point out people in the community who have led exemplary lives.
- Make an effort to have children attend a family reunion, and find ways for them to visit with relatives, friends, or community members who encourage students to do their best.
- Assign children responsibilities at home to foster independence, self-reliance, and resourcefulness.
- Teach planning skills by requiring children to complete homework and household chores before play.
- Acknowledge and reward children for good behavior and performance; also, correct misconduct.
- Realize that some children may be under peer pressure not to excel academically; strong parental support can help them resist this pressure not to excel.

Parent-Friendly Support

In the 1994 Gallup poll, at least 70% of the citizens surveyed thought the general breakdown in the American family structure contributed to the causes of violence in the nation's schools (Elam, Rose, & Gallup, 1994). If nontraditional family structures lead to school violence, then parents are being criticized indirectly for the violent acts in our schools. Such criticism will not erase the various family structures in which students live. These include first marriages, single parenthood, remarriages, and cohabitation partnerships. The family structure is just as diverse as the student population.

Parent-friendly schools will not fault students for their family lifestyle; instead, they will nurture the role parents can play in education. Schools have to do more to reach out, assist, and inform parents. The need for such support is likely to be strong in families with lower levels of education and one-parent households. In extending support to parents, school personnel can provide orientations that supply information about the following:

- A code for peaceful conduct, including standards of behavior, disciplinary measures, and the penalties for misconduct. The code should be in the form of a performance contract for parents to sign and return, acknowledging that they, too, understand the standards for peaceful behavior.

- Policies regarding student dismissal, sick days, tardiness, and special permission
- School expectations and attendance requirements
- Important dates (e.g., report card dates, parent-teacher conference dates, vacation and holiday dates, teacher inservice days, home visit dates, etc.)
- Topics being covered in class, to foster parent-child communication about school
- Learning activities and questions teachers would like to have parents respond to with their children as part of a family-centered project
- Visiting while school is in session, and social events in which parents and teachers can become acquainted in a friendly, informal setting
- Telephone tutoring services, in which someone is available to assist students having difficulty with class assignments
- School events that emphasize the value of education and the conviction that all children can learn in a calm, safe environment

Parental support needs to continue throughout the school year as it is important to student achievement. Likewise, schools can remind parents to reniforce their child's commitment to education by posting or printing the following guidelines.

ABC's for Parenthood

A   *Always let your children know they are important members of the family.*
B   *Be willing to make time for them to talk about problems and share ideas with you.*
C   *Commend their good behavior.*
D   *Display your affection each day with kisses, hugs, and positive expressions.*
E   *Emphasize the "Golden Rule"—Teach them to treat others as they wish to be treated.*
F   *Find ways for them to feel good about themselves.*

G   Guide their motivation to learn at school and at home.

H   Help them deal with fears, phobias, and negative feelings.

I   Include their options in matters related to family decision making.

J   Join them in doing the things they like.

K   Keep their trust.

L   Listen and contemplate when they say, "You're not being fair."

M   Mend disagreements in a way that teaches them to compromise.

N   Notice their needs and protect them from harm.

O   On occasion, surprise them by doing something special.

P   Praise them for thoughtful and kind deeds.

Q   Question their interest in social fads.

R   Remember they are young and sometimes confused by the adult world.

S   Show them where you work and what you do.

T   Try not to criticize them for mistakes caused by inexperience.

U   Understand their need for love and approval.

V   Value your dreams for them to have life-long goals.

W   Warn them about the consequences of breaking rules.

X   Expect them to give you truthful answers.

Y   Yield to their choices, if they agree with your principles.

Z   Zealously prepare children to become productive members of society.

Parent-Teacher Conferences

Parent-teacher conferences allow families and schools to work together in creating and supporting rich academic experiences for children. These meetings serve as a basis for parents' involvement in the educational development of their children. They are described here as hostile, ineffective, or informative.

Hostile conferences are power struggles between parents and teachers. They are the direct result of poor communications, status conflicts, personal confrontations, attributing blame, or the weak application of interpersonal skills. Hostilities usually occur when people are threatened, are embarrassed, or sense they are being taken advantage of, judged unfairly, or controlled. Hostile conferences represent a "lose-lose" situation in which neither party departs from the table with a plan to help the child succeed in school.

Ineffective conferences waste time and opportunities for collaboration. They may cause teachers to form misconceptions about a child's homelife, especially when lines of communication for building a supportive home-school relationship are difficult to establish with parents. At times, ineffective or unproductive conferences are the result of poor planning, confusion, and the failure to listen to the concerns of each party.

Informative conferences have a set agenda or established purpose. They are conducted in a friendly, nonthreatening, businesslike manner with parents and teachers having an equal stake in the conference's success. Responsive and open to the other's ideas, the individuals communicate effectively while keeping the child's interests at the forefront of the discussion. Such conferences provide a possible plan of action to promote the child's academic and personal achievement and provide suggestions that parents and teachers can use to help the child overcome weaknesses. Informative conferences generally offer parents and teachers an opportunity to work together for the child's school success.

To ensure that parent-teacher conferences are successful, the following suggestions may help.

1. Establish a working relationship with parents early in the academic year, as the initial contact should be positive.
2. Use telephone calls, personal notes, and information sheets to keep parents up-to-date on the learning goals, objectives, and activities covered in class.
3. Set up meeting times that are responsive to working schedules and personal responsibilities.
4. Reduce the uncertainties and anxieties of parents by establishing the purpose of the meeting before they attend.
5. Remind parents of the meeting time and location shortly before the meeting is to take place.
6. Create a summary sheet to review conference goals, purposes, and expected outcomes. Also, gather necessary documents to present a portfolio of the child's performances and behaviors in school. Have an agenda that allows the meeting to be timely, well organized, and task oriented.
7. Greet parents in a pleasant manner when they arrive. Remind them of the purposes established for the meeting.

8. Listen reflectively to parent's concerns and comments. Resist temptations to place blame; instead, make an attempt to empathize with the parents' struggle to assist their children. Try to remove blame from the discussion by focusing on ways to help improve the child's academic success.

9. Communicate in a clear and concise manner and avoid the use of educational jargon. Be sensitive to the real or perceived status differences between parents and educators by using "we" and not "you" in your conversation.

10. Focus on a plan of action to build on the child's strengths and alleviate learning weaknesses.

11. Use a problem-solving model to help parents understand issues and explore choices and possible solutions. Offer information on support services that can be beneficial. Be timely and offer realistic outcomes.

12. End parent conferences on a positive note.

Closing Thoughts

Although educators and parents set goals for a safe, orderly school, parents serve as role models for peace. Moreover, parents are their children's first teachers. Children learn how to function in the world by observing and imitating them. They learn how to deal with personal conflicts, establish relationships, tackle challenges, and achieve goals according to the models adults provide.

Occasionally parents may feel uneasy talking to school personnel whose knowledge about the educational process exceeds their own. Their dismissal of past school disappointments and discouragements may add to the child's performance. Overall, administrators and teachers must make an effort to help parents enhance the learning and teaching of children.

Let's Talk

1. What kind of obstacles do teachers encounter in working with parents?

2. In your opinion, how can schools be oriented more toward parents and families?

3. What kind of assistance should be provided for parents unable to attend parent-teacher conferences?

4. What can parents do at home to teach children how to behave peacefully?

5. What kind of school activities promote good parent-teacher relationships?

Suggested Activities

1. Prepare a list of recommendations to help the home and the school contribute to the success of the problem teenagers mentioned in this chapter (see p. 88).

2. Read the school-parent activities in Table 6.1 (see p. 97) and identify additional activities you would like to propose for your school.

3. Read the family routines in Table 6.2 (see p. 98), then list several more you would like to propose for use in a monthly home achievement packet.

4. Help your school prepare a parent handbook that includes information describing how the school is sensitive to diverse family structures, values, and needs of students.

5. Develop a parent workshop on parent-child communication for a peaceful home environment.

6. List what you consider to be the 10 most important activities for successful family-school partnerships. Then, use the list to determine the kinds of activities that could be implemented in your school.

7. Plan and present a skit in which you encourage parents to become actively involved in their children's education.

Table 6.1 School-Parent Activities

Open House

For some parents, the school open-house program may be their first and only contact with the school during the year. Make it a night to remember. Have students prepare a special welcome message for parents, and if possible, prepare a videotape to show parents what students did the first few weeks of school.

Weekly Progress Notes

Send home individual behavioral notes prepared and delivered by students every Friday. Inside, have a statement and four items to rate student behavior —e.g., my classroom citizenship for the week was: (a) excellent, (b) good, (c) fair, (d) poor—and a place for the teacher's and parents' signatures.

Telephone Connection

Each week, the teacher calls a parent with some positive information about his or her child (e.g., "Just wanted to let you know that Billy was selected as a peer mediator"). If the parent does not have a telephone, a postcard with the same information will work as well.

Class Newsletter

Send class newsletters home, prepared and delivered by students, at least once every 2 months to keep parents up-to-date on events in school. Be sure the newsletter includes as many students' names as possible.

New Meeting Hours

Set parent-teacher activity schedules to accommodate working parents and teachers at the end of a tiring day. Start the meetings at a convenient early hour so participants can be home at 8:30 instead of 10:00 p.m. Bring finger food so no one sits through the meeting hungry.

At-Home Meetings

Ask a parent to act as host and invite neighbors to meet school leaders and teachers. An informal at-home meeting helps promote school-parent rapport. Ask members of the group to present ideas for family-school-community partnerships.

Table 6.2 Family Routines

Simple routines can give children a sense of security, stability, and family life. Families most often celebrate holidays and establish traditions, such as birthdays. However, in the rush of everyday life, it is more difficult to keep in place the small, daily routines that provide family continuity. The Egleston Children's Hospital Center for Child Advocacy (1992) suggests the following ideas for small routines:

Reading to your child at bedtime is a peaceful, soothing way to close an active day. Even 10 or 15 minutes of reading aloud can become an anticipated ritual that children will learn to use as a way to relax, share some time with a parent, and feel special.

Sit down to meals together. This gives the family time to communicate about the day. It does not have to be an elaborate meal or every night of the week. Designate one night of the week as family night; take the phone off the hook and spend time together. Breakfast may be easier to have together if evenings are busy.

Reinforce the parent-child connection with simple words and actions that are unique to your family. Saying, "I love you," to your children before bedtime or as the first greeting of the day tells them how special they are.

Play games with your children. This gives them the sense that you enjoy spending time with them. The games can be simple ones invented by you, or a board game, a singing game, or sports.

Cook with your child for a fun, easy way to spend time together and establish routines. Helping in the kitchen also teaches a child responsibility and develops skills. Children love to be in a helping role, and you are creating memories at the same time.

Take pictures for a simple, memorable way to create routines. Family photographs can be very powerful in reconstructing memories and bringing back the feelings attached to an event or a moment.

Storytelling is an activity that can be done anywhere. The story can be about a parent's childhood or can include the child as one of the characters. Children enjoy contributing part of the story or guessing the ending.

Performing family chores and errands can make children feel as if they are making a significant contribution to the family. Take one child with you as you do errands. This gives both of you a chance to have individual time together if he or she has brothers or sisters.

Going on family outings is a way to build memories and routines. These can be one-day adventures or an annual family vacation.

PRINCIPLE 7:

The family-school-community partnerships should implement peacebuilding programs to further the development of harmony among people.

∽ 7 ∼

Building Family-School-
Community Partnerships

*Many children are growing up healthy, resilient, and skilled,
but too many are not. Violence and poverty, poor health, teen
parenthood, and school failure dim the future of millions of
children. And when their future is dimmed, the lives of all
Americans are diminished.*

Center for the Study
of Social Policy (1993, p. 2).

For the millions of children failing to meet the challenges of education, their health and social and economic well-being must be everyone's concern. When they attend school abused, hungry, neglected, or unhappy, these emotional, physical, and social needs require attention. School personnel have to invite organizations and agencies to assist in providing services to deal with the complex problems that go beyond the academic realm. The call for change to benefit the lives of children inside and outside the school environment (American Psychological Association [APA] Commission, 1993) is critical. It is essential for social service agencies to respond to this call by helping schools serve the human needs and learning needs of children.

School-Community Social Services

Family-school-community partnerships that serve troubled students through collaborative school-community social services are based on the concept of the "school as a community center." The intent is to meet the needs of families and children by combining the bureaucratic formalities of social services into an efficient, comprehensive, and integrated system designed to handle the many problems related to teenage pregnancy, drug abuse, juvenile crime, adolescent suicide, and the AIDS epidemic.

Although schools participate as one of the many entities in a social service center, organizing a program model to fit and remedy the unique needs of children involves planning. Because urban, suburban, and rural communities differ, there are no simple explanations or blueprints to organize a center, obtain funding, or seek additional resources.

School districts where centers are mandated (e.g., New Jersey, Iowa, Kentucky) may differ from those with voluntary programs. Whether providing involuntary or voluntary programs, schools continue to employ the professionals needed for crisis intervention, counseling, and psychological services. These services generally include therapeutic activities for children who have been injured by violence or witnessed an unusual violent event. For example, the social service staff members may have a role in removing children from an unsafe home environment or visiting the home to keep them from being victims of violence.

When children witness violence, they suffer from anger, fear, hopelessness, confusion, or irrational thinking. Sad to say, "schools have become the emergency room of emotions, devoted not only to developing minds but also to repairing hearts" (McClellan, 1994, p. 2). Emergency room duty is not a teaching function but it is a humanitarian function. The inclusion of such duties and responsibilities in daily school life is now viewed as the therapeutic curriculum.

Such a curriculum does exist in elementary schools with collaborative school-community social services. One case where health, welfare, governmental, and community agencies have joined the private and business sectors in providing social services at the school site is the Fourth Street Elementary School in Athens, GA (Gantt, 1992). This award-winning school-community program does more than educate children; it offers family counseling services and education activities for parents.

School-based social services establish links among agencies that affect students and their parents, handle the coordination and networking for total services to families, plan and implement long-term intervention strategies, and use a proactive approach to serve the educational and social needs of children. State and community agencies in the school building offer support for the tutoring, counseling, child care, health, family activities, and parent education services. These collaborative services have a positive influence on students, families, and the community.

Family-Community-School Collaboration

There are different forms of collaboration appropriate for arranging family-community-school networks. The local needs make it necessary for school personnel to determine the type of collaboration appropriate to serve students, families, and members of the community effectively. Logically, the collaboration should accommodate the school as it works to enrich the learning and achievement of youngsters whose lifestyle, culture, and ethnic background differ.

The six types of collaboration developed by Joyce Epstein (1992) can help school personnel identify, plan, and implement family-community-school networks. The various levels of collaboration shown are vital to the improvement of schools and student outcomes. In addition, they provide some ideas about what to expect from each type.

Six Types of Collaboration

School Help for Families. Assistance is provided by the school to help families with basic obligations: responsibility for their children's health and safety; supervision, discipline, and guidance for children at each age level; and positive home conditions that support school learning and behavior appropriate for each grade level.

School-Home Communication. The basic obligation of schools communicating with the home about school programs and children's progress includes the use of letters, memos, phone calls, report cards, newsletters, conferences, and other mechanisms.

Parent-Community Help for Schools. The involvement of parents and community volunteers assists teachers, administrators, and children in classrooms and other areas of the school. Parents and others visit the school to support and watch student performances, sports, and other events.

Learning Activities at Home. In response to parent- or child-initiated requests for help, these are, particularly, ideas from teachers for parents to monitor or assist their children at home in learning activities that can be coordinated with classroom instruction.

Governance, Decision Making, and Advocacy. Parents and other community residents are involved in advisory, decision-making, or advocacy roles in parent associations, advisory committees, and school improvement or school site councils. Also, parent and community activists participate in independent advocacy groups that monitor the schools or work for school improvement.

Community Collaboration and Exchanges. This refers to the involvement of any of the institutions or agencies that share some responsibility for children's development and success. This includes programs that coordinate and provide access to community support services for children and their families and other arrangements that draw on community resources to support children's learning.

The type of collaboration successful to your school's commitment to involve a family-community-school unit may or may not accommodate comprehensive exchanges, but it should include a link between school and social services. In some communities, the building of collaborative networks will need to include outreach programs that can help youths separated from the mainstream: the homeless, runaways, school dropouts, or juvenile delinquents. Such programs should offer services to youths who engage in high-risk behaviors (gang fights, drug use or dealing, alcohol abuse, or criminal acts) as well as juvenile offenders in need of counseling services.

Youth and Crime

It is normal for concerned citizens to expect the police and criminal justice system to reduce the crimes committed in their community.

Yet much of the violence that occurs does not take place in a criminal setting; it occurs between companions involved in arguments, sometimes over trivial matters (National Center for Injury Prevention and Control [NCIPC], 1993). This is the reason it seems logical to teach students conflict resolution management and strategies to avoid arguments and fights, preventing them from becoming either the criminal or the victim.

When conflict resolution management is practiced, it can help deter violence but only if youths learn to replace their anger and hostility with nonviolent behaviors. Encouraging them to change from old to new behaviors requires time and repeated use of peacemaking skills. Acquisition of such skills remains an individual effort, within a home and community environment supportive of peacemaking. Also critical to peacemaking is the student's attitude, as the person must want to modify his or her conduct.

Schools and communities should be concerned about youths who need special assistance to help modify high-risk behaviors, especially those who have a predisposition to become involved in violence and criminal activities later in life. They are the youngsters, 10 years old or less, who have been victimized through abuse, neglect, or exploitation (NCIPC, 1993). By age 13, they may be committing serious property crimes in addition to experiencing difficulties in school.

Juvenile crimes peak between the ages of 16 and 17, yet most career criminals are not identified until approximately age 22. This information reported by the Office of Juvenile Justice and Delinquency Prevention (1993) shows that youths with habitual crime records continue their violence against people. They have become the "invisible delinquents" attending school with other students. When incidents committed by juvenile offenders (assaults, burglaries, petty theft or shoplifting, or attempted suicide) are not reported to school officials, teachers and principals have no knowledge of the students' record.

Violent youths are officially invisible to the community at large until they commit an extremely serious crime. School personnel, however, can watch for signs of troubled youth by maintaining records of student misconduct, suspensions, and expulsions. A detailed roster on behavioral problems will help reveal the nature of juvenile activities. This kind of record keeping is a way for social services to assist students who show early patterns of chronic behavior that may lead to habitual crime.

Profiles containing information relevant to a juvenile's offending behavior, including criminal and traffic arrest history, case summaries, descriptive data, modus operandi, police information, drug or alcohol involvement, social behavior, and school history, are recommended by the SHOCAP Program (Serious Habitual Offender Comprehensive Action Program, 1994). It is a profile system that encourages the school system, police department, juvenile probation department, youth services, and agencies in the juvenile justice system to share information in order to make informed decisions about youth and crime.

In some communities, school detectives have responsibility for the management of juvenile crime information and analysis. Their duties may also include teaching subjects related to law and violence, counseling students, policing school grounds, providing law enforcement, or school-police public relations. They help to improve school safety as well as provide supervision, security, and delinquency prevention.

Delinquency: What Are the Causes?

Why do some individuals want to destroy the social peace that others work so hard to preserve? Parents and community residents have speculative views on the causes of crime, but among educators there is the view that crime is a learned behavior. They tend to think students learn criminal behavior through interaction with peers who defy the law. There is also the notion that youths who see themselves as delinquents behave according to their negative self-image.

According to Pelfrey (1993), juvenile delinquency is influenced by many factors, and no one perspective or theory can be considered the "correct" explanation. His story about the judge, the mother, the police officer, and the teacher questioning the causes of hostile behavior in the following courtroom scenario indicates a need to find answers regarding the causes of delinquency.

Juvenile in Court

The Judge

Trying to interpret the youth's hostility, the judge stared at the young man in front of him. Was he as uncaring as his record indicated? Had he been influenced by other wiser and more mature offenders? Why had he engaged in these seemingly senseless criminal acts? Is society to blame? Is this young man salvageable? As the judge drummed his fingers on the desk top, he realized that he had ample facts concerning the youth's offenses but only guesses concerning the causes of his behavior.

The Mother

The young man's mother sat tensely, watching the judge and her son. She had not been surprised when told that her son was in the detention center and, thinking back, she had even anticipated that call. She had tried so hard and failed so miserably with this child that it was almost as if he were destined to do the things he had done. Had she caused his behavior? Was it unfair to this child and to her other children to have divorced and given him only a one-parent home? Had she been too lenient? Too strict? What could she have done differently? What could she do differently in the future? No answers, only guesses.

The Police Officer

The police officer had seen scenes like this unfold many times. This young man had been stoic during his arrest and hearings. Others took different tactics and used apologies, confessions, and tears to cleanse their souls or manipulate the system. Only a seasoned observer could guess at the different motives. Had the die been cast with this young man? Is there any hope for his future?

The Teacher

A caring teacher willing to expend hours of extra work with problem children may be a rarity in many school systems today. Such a teacher sat in the audience and sadly watched the proceedings. This young man had potential, the capability to do well, but he had chosen other ways to define success. Could she have motivated him another way? Could she have spent more time with him and stimulated his interest in academic success? Could she have trained him to defer gratification and think to the future? Could she have seen this coming and referred him to others within the school system more capable of handling his problems?

As they looked for answers, did the thoughts and questions of individuals in the courtroom scenario overlook the possibility that this young man alone was responsible for his behavior—that he had freely chosen to commit the offenses? The answers to all of their questions as well as this last one could be yes—or no—or maybe. Every person interested in this young man's situation tried to understand his or her role in causing or altering his behavior. Cooperative efforts between family, school, and the juvenile justice system to find solutions will have to include the development of innovative approaches.

For instance, judges could do more than decide the sentencing appropriate to fit the crime. When juveniles are allowed to go back to school following a court hearing, judges should not only insist that they return to school but also lecture them about getting good grades, attending school every day, being prepared to learn, and setting long-term educational goals. The school system has to consider how teachers and staff members will treat students who have been arrested or charged with a crime. Measures should be taken to keep them from becoming repeat offenders. Such measures would mean more cooperation between the school system and social service agencies to provide counseling, an expanded alternative school curriculum, and additional family education activities.

Special provisions and programs for juveniles to examine the role models and influences in their life (e.g., peers, family members, teachers, community leaders, etc.) may offer the insight they need to explore the causes of and elements that contribute to their behavior. Furthermore, if they are coerced to conduct criminal activities through their association with others, it is imperative for them to understand how their interaction with individuals who commit crimes can have a negative effect on their future.

Denying Problems

Stop fretting about juvenile crime, take two sugar pills, and wait a decade for it to go away. (Crowe, 1994, p. 21)

It's absurd for anyone to wait for crime to disappear when so many communities, whether rich or poor, large or small, now have problems. If individuals have not had others threaten or harm them, or for some reason think they are free from crime, their sense of violence is abstract. Although crime may not be an immediate concern in every community, procedures to handle violent situations should be a concern for school personnel. Organizing a crisis management plan to cope with an unexpected incident or crisis is essential (see p. 21).

Administrators who deny or refuse to accept the presence of violence in their schools fail to realize the need for a plan to prevent or manage disruptions. Part of admitting that a crisis is possible involves assessing the school's preparedness. In talking to administrators about crime, the chairman of the National Association of School Safety and Law Enforcement Officers reports that some administrators will say, "Thank God, I don't have that problem." But, when it does happen, they call to ask, "How do I deal with this?" (Ordovensky, 1993, p. 22).

When school personnel have no idea how to respond appropriately to violent situations, it can lead to confusion among students, faculty and staff members, parents, and community residents. The confusion can cause panic and delays in notifying intervention agencies such as the police department, hospital, social services, and community groups. Denying problems that may lead to an emergency situation does little to help educators, parents, and concerned citizens be proactive against the societal violence spilling over into the school.

Family-School-Community Action Plan

An action plan to create a framework for peace starts with bringing a group of individuals together to share their views about families, schools, and communities. They should represent agencies willing to combine efforts with diverse organizations and groups to establish a peacebuilding program at the community level. Activities related to the development of an action plan will require the support and resources of private organizations, governmental agencies, and local businesses.

Gathering ideas and issues for the group to discuss can be obtained by surveying the opinions of community residents at supermarkets, malls, recreational areas, churches, schools, universities, and homes. Survey findings can help the group identify needs, missions, and strategies that are realistic and appropriate for the community.

Family-school-community peacebuilding groups may choose to adopt some of these action plan strategies or create their own. Some of the school-related strategies suggested by a group representing various entities and institutions in the DeKalb County (1994) community are included in the following mission statements.

Mission 1—School-Community Involvement

Suggested Strategies

– Conduct a school/community assessment to identify, define, and prioritize peacebuilding and violence prevention needs.
– Form a focus group on the prevention of violence. Invite pediatricians, dentists, psychiatrists, psychologists, psychotherapists, lawyers, judges, school board members, college/university professors, social workers, nurses, police officers, parents, students, administrators, teachers, community leaders, etc.
– Develop a family-school-community action plan identifying the goals, objectives, methods, and activities to implement a peacebuilding program.
– Involve all segments of the community in a peacebuilding program by inviting everyone to work together to find ways to prevent violence.
– Keep the community informed about progress to fulfill program goals and provide immediate suggestions on ways to fight violence and crime. For example, one immediate suggestion would be for parents to become familiar with neighbors and their children.

Mission 2—School-Neighborhood Improvement

Suggested Strategies

– Promote school-neighborhood pride, safety, and security to prevent students and school personnel from being fearful of the environment outside the school building.
– Invite residents near the school to participate in a nighttime school watch program by reporting any unusual activity at the school to the police.

- Ask community residents and businesses to volunteer their places as "safe places" where children can go if they are threatened while walking to and from school or waiting at the bus stop. These locations can have signs posted in their windows designating them as safe places, but volunteers should be screened closely before they are included in the program.
- Conduct programs to reduce weapons and drugs, increase neighborhood watch patrols, and expand school and community drug-free zones.
- Encourage neighborhood participation in school beautification and community development projects.

Mission 3—School Enrichment Activities

Suggested Strategies

- Plan year-round enrichment activities as outlets for students' stress and anger; also provide opportunities for social interaction and problem solving. Enrichment programs might include activities on Fridays and Saturdays. During the week, after normal school hours, plan special events for families to spend quality time together.
- Use school facilities and other facilities in the community such as recreation centers for afterschool classes, school programs, and violence prevention programs. The facilities could be available to all community-based organizations and agencies that meet the needs of children and their families.
- Recruit adults in the neighborhood to create and lead afterschool youth clubs, community athletic teams, and other recreational programs.

Mission 4—Services for Parents

Suggested Strategies

- Offer support for parents to learn nonviolent methods of child care, discipline, and home management. Implement an early childhood violence prevention program that will provide advanced training for professional child care workers and parents.

- Provide services to parents by sponsoring classes regularly in schools and community facilities. If possible, make parents' attendance at a parenting class a prerequisite to a child's enrollment in preschool or kindergarten.
- Provide child care for parents taking classes and conduct classes in a variety of locations (e.g., clinics, schools, youth centers, apartment complexes). Use incentives to increase parent participation and attendance (e.g., telephone certificates, savings bonds).
- Expand parent services to include the following activities: parenting skills, survival skills, counseling, health services, conflict resolution training, study habits and practices for children, and tutorials for G.E.D courses.

Mission 5—Youth Employment

Suggested Strategies

- Design curriculum to include work study and coop classes for high school students and vocational-technical training for middle school students. Offer ongoing job and skill training for youths (dropouts and high-risk students) to become productive employees.
- Encourage counselors to assist students with job search skills. Ask businesses in the community to hire local youths, create incentives for hiring youths, conduct job marketing campaigns for youth employment, support adopt-a-student programs, organize apprenticeship programs, and enhance any programs that currently serve the same function.
- Set up summer youth work programs, training for existing jobs, and training for self-employment strategies.

Mission 6—Youth Services

Suggested Strategies

- Form a centralized database of all youth organizations and youth development programs in the community. Organize a community-wide referral service to communicate available resources and services to all youth-serving agencies.

- Raise community awareness regarding youth-related violence as being everyone's concern. Arrange to have a referral hotline telephone number for troubled and delinquent youths to call.
- Employ more school counselors to help implement programs for youth and to assist in the areas of emotional and social development.
- Involve youths in the planning of programs to develop themselves in areas that will help them in adult life and impress on them the need for lifelong learning.
- Teach life skills to youths (e.g., empathy training, positive communication, leadership and peacemaking skills, work ethics, stress management, sportsmanship, financial management, coping skills, listening skills, self-respect, self-discipline, etc.).

Mission 7—Juvenile Justice System

Suggested Strategies

- Help the juvenile system better respond to modern criminal violence. Seek ways for Juvenile Court judges to be creative regarding the sentencing of juvenile offenders (e.g., consider house arrest, electronic monitoring, community service, longer sentences where appropriate, funds for alternative sentencing, volunteer professional counseling, professional training programs).
- Provide better control of juveniles repeatedly convicted of delinquent and unruly offenses (e.g., truancy, curfew violations, substance abuse). Repeat offenders could be mandated to a counseling or mentoring program. If convicted for violent crimes, they should not be protected by confidentiality.
- Set mandatory limits on probation and social service cases to facilitate thorough follow-up with repeat offenders. School systems and the Juvenile Court system should consider developing services for truants and runaways. Also, consider stricter enforcement of state and school truancy laws.

Mission 8—Changing Values and Attitudes

Suggested Strategies

- Foster respect among all community members and provide them with skills to resolve conflict in a nonviolent manner. Saturate the community with programs and learning opportunities for children and adults.
- Promote the importance of education, school, and family. Organize school mentoring programs for youth, as they need positive role models. Sponsor activities to support family love, respect, compassion, honesty, unity, and responsibility.
- Offer programs for school personnel, parents, and concerned citizens to understand the values and attitudes of diverse racial and ethnic groups in the community. Emphasize the need for members of the family-school-community to respect the beliefs of other people, to value themselves as individuals, and to accept each other.

Mission 9—School Policies

Suggested Strategies

- Review school policies to determine whether current practices are realistic in meeting the needs of students in today's society. For example, policies related to employment of personnel, class size, staffing and scheduling, testing procedures, and health services should be reviewed for changes.
- Provide appropriate alternatives for youths who get suspended from school. Revise policies to ensure that they do not get into trouble while suspended. A few suggestions might be: ongoing school work requirements for suspended students, in-school suspensions at alternative schools, community service work, a mentoring program, or a follow-up program.

Closing Thoughts

School personnel have the ability to solicit family and community support in peacebuilding efforts so that children attend safe, drug-free, and violence-free schools. Making use of community resources and services to improve education starts with the philosophy that local residents and parents have to model the social peace they want students to learn. Efforts to prevent the hostility, destruction, and harm suffered by children and youths must be everyone's concern. Together, the powerful elements of family-school-community partnerships can reduce the fear of violence and strengthen the practice of peace.

Let's Talk

1. What is the relationship between your school and social service agencies in the community?
2. How do child protection services and youth services work with students and teachers at your school?
3. To what extent do the school administrators, school detectives, juvenile courts, corrections, human services, prosecution, and other public or private agencies work together to keep juveniles from becoming repeat offenders?
4. Describe the crisis management plan faculty, staff members, and students should follow if an unexpected emergency or violent incident occurs at your school.
5. Identify the types of collaborative family-school-community partnerships currently in progress at your school.
6. What are some of the problems a school-home-community peacebuilding program might be able to solve for teachers and administrators?

Suggested Activities

1. Write a set of procedures to describe how you would want architects to design future schools to facilitate family-school-community partnerships.

2. Prepare a list of the various social, human, and medical service agencies in your community that can help school personnel understand students' needs and problems.

3. Write a position paper or prepare a speech on the topic, "Peacebuilding in Our Community."

4. Prepare a chart outlining the activities you would want to conduct to include teachers, parents, students, community residents, colleges and universities, organizations, agencies, businesses, and the news media in the development of an action plan for peace.

5. Prepare several suggestions for school personnel to consider in the effort to resolve some of the causes and problems created by students who are at high risk of expulsion, suspension, or dropping out of school.

6. Develop an information guide for youths who dropped out to encourage them to think about returning to school as a way to increase their chance of being productive, healthy citizens.

SUGGESTED RESOURCES

Peace is rarely denied to the peaceful.
Johann von Schiller

This section provides information on resources that can be beneficial to individuals interested in materials on (a) elementary curriculum, (b) secondary curriculum, (c) programs and curriculum guides, (d) family-school-community resources, (e) resource organizations, (f) theme-based literature, (g) children's books, and (h) professional books.

Resource A: Social Peace Curriculum for Primary and Elementary Schools

A social curriculum for young children should provide opportunities for them to express themselves peacefully, share responsibilities with classmates, and care for their surroundings. The following is a list of suggested skills, activities, and ideas for teachers to consider.

Environmental learning activities might offer opportunities for children to:

- Clean up after themselves.
- Dispose of trash and unwanted food properly.
- Use supplies, equipment, and materials correctly.
- Be careful when handling glass or breakable items.
- Walk and move around the class in an orderly manner.
- Pass through the halls quietly without distracting others.
- Alert a teacher when an accident or an emergency occurs.
- Keep papers, folders, and books in order.

Cooperative activities can focus on positive behaviors and include skills for children to:

- Assist the teacher.
- Be supportive and kind to a new student.
- Offer help to someone in trouble.
- Ask for permission to use items that belong to someone else.
- Share their possessions with others.
- Ask others to play on the playground.
- Be fair and wait their turn when playing a game.
- Compromise in settling disagreements or disputes.

Activities that emphasize communication skills can encourage children to:

- Let one person talk while others listen.
- Raise their hand and be recognized by the teacher before speaking.
- Greet peers, classmates, and teachers by name.
- Introduce themselves to others in a proper manner.
- Use a friendly tone of voice.
- Walk away from arguments that might lead to a fight.
- Tell the teacher about verbal insults and physical assaults.

Curriculum activities related to moral and ethical decisions might include information that teaches children to:

- Answer questions truthfully.
- Think constructively.
- Oppose the use of profane language.
- Respect the racial and cultural background of classmates.
- Know and follow classroom rules.
- Apologize for inappropriate actions.

Additional information for primary and elementary teachers interested in teaching positive social behavior can be found in the Appendix, Resource C: Annotated List of Programs and Curriculum Guides for Peaceful Schools.

Resource B: Social Peace
Curriculum for Middle and High School

Teaching middle and high school students to enhance peace, learn responsibility, and use behavior management to prevent disruptions and conflicts are a few of the goals recommended for a social peace curriculum. Different curriculum programs and guidelines (see Resource C) on topics that contribute to peace (e.g., social skills, self-discipline, conflict resolution, character education, and values clarification) include various forms of information for use in planning and designing curricula.

Curriculum Design

A social peace curriculum should represent innovative ways to address peace as a subject and as a practice. It can be designed to help students succeed academically and expand the school's role of helping students develop social responsibility. To create a curriculum to build and sustain peacemaking in schools, curriculum developers and teachers may select themes and topics with the students' interests in mind.

For example, students might have an interest in studying (a) funds allocated and spent for security (math), (b) forms of violence in print and other media (English), (c) fear of victimization (psychology), (d) physical injuries (health education), (e) criminal violations and laws (civics), (f) communicable diseases (science), and (g) crime statistical data-bases (computer science).

Problem Solving

It is important to teach students to solve problems in the process of learning. In Chapter 5, both the eight-step problem-solving approach and the action plan problem-solving approach are presented. They are appropriate for a social peace curriculum in any subject area because they prepare students to plan and think about solutions to academic and personal problems. One particular use for these methods is for students to make decisions about classroom discipline management systems and the consequences of disobeying rules.

Another use for problem-solving is for students to learn the causes, immediate effects, and long-term implications of school violence and conflicts. Such an approach is practical for students' use in determining through a student court system what happens to classmates who violate school rules. As part of a court system, they can establish peaceful codes of behavior and standards that address student conduct and responsibility.

Content Areas

The information that follows suggests content area ideas to consider in developing a social peace curriculum for mathematics and technology, science, health education, physical education, English, history, music, and art.

Mathematics and Technology

- Use math and technological applications to study mass transportation systems, construction of energy efficient homes and automobiles, and strategies to build global communities through technology.
- Find ways for students to come in contact with men and women who use mathematical and technological skills. They should

see positive role models and concrete examples showing the importance of math skills.

- Have students use their math skills to survey, analyze, and report on peace issues. Math and computer skills can be combined to project the cost benefits of conducting community service projects (e.g., aluminum can collections, food and clothing donations, used book sales).

Science

- Organize lessons for students to study the scientific discoveries and inventions that have improved our quality of life (e.g., polio vaccine, blood plasma, chemotherapy).
- Plan for students to develop their own inventions to address human needs. Have them discuss ethical and moral issues related to the ways science can prolong and destroy life on earth (e.g., radiation, ozone depletion, global warming, chemical warfare).
- Encourage students to read about the discoveries and inventions made by people of all racial and ethnic groups, and conduct research on famous inventors to dramatize their roles in helping humankind. Help students understand that curiosity is not relegated to certain racial or ethnic groups.

Health Education

- Explore economic, political, and social factors that affect medical research and pharmacokinetic efforts to find cures for fatal diseases.
- Discuss information about the significant role health organizations and worldwide institutions play in sharing resources, managing population crisis, and handling medical emergencies (e.g., World Health Organization, World Bank, Doctors Without Borders, Red Cross).
- Encourage students to form a school group or association to address local health issues, and medical concerns.

Physical Education

- Emphasize the students' personal health and well-being by teaching them to care for their physical as well as mental health. They can sponsor a health and physical education fair to deal with health, stress, and wellness issues.
- Present lessons about proper nutrition and exercise for each developmental stage of physical growth. Also, recognize the importance of cooperation, competition, leisure activities, and the need for recognition in everyone's life.

English

- Select literature that will enrich students' lives, promote positive self-esteem, and be future oriented.
- Maintain a collection of magazine articles, books, short stories, and newspaper clippings on achievement, overcoming adversities, and developing friendships to highlight a "Story of the Week or Month."
- Help students produce a social peace publication to reflect the diverse ideas and cultures represented in their school. It could be used to instill school pride and peaceful relations and to recognize the students' voice in school affairs.
- Plan activities for students to submit book reviews and articles about persistence, humor, success, conflict resolution, career awareness, and higher education information about scholarships and grants to the school newspaper.

History

- Have students explore history from the perspective of positive social interactions and communities working to build the United States. Assign teams of students to research different racial, ethnic, or religious groups and explore their contributions to American history.
- Prepare lessons for students to study the contributions of many groups who have been marginalized in history (e.g., Chinese immigrants who built the railroads to provide for westward expansion).

- Present historical figures and heroes who sought to promote peaceful resolutions to conflicts.
- Organize history content to consistently include the peacemakers throughout history as well as information on wars, conflicts, battles, and migrations important to the development of global microcultures.

Music

- Study the songs, music, and dance created to remember the pain and suffering of political prisoners, frightened refugees, and communities in war zones.
- Have students compose and record antiviolence and peacemaking music. Allow students to present their musical compositions and dance routines during assemblies.

Peace Art Center

- Establish a peace art center in the school building to highlight student efforts to build and sustain peace. The center can be an outlet for students' artwork, poetry, music, action plans, inspirational messages, and literary works. Arrange for the center to have a meeting area to resolve disputes, conduct group discussions, and exchange ideas.
- Prepare a peace calendar to acknowledge the days throughout history on which (a) conflicts were resolved, (b) peaceful actions were recognized, (c) peacemakers were born, (d) children's celebrations were held, and (e) human rights and policies were established.

Peacemaking Skills

Reinforcing the students' willingness to learn and use peacemaking skills starts with the teacher's commitment, integrity, and fairness. Students need to explore the appropriateness of their choices in a warm, caring, and nonjudgmental environment. It is necessary for a social peace curriculum to include opportunities for them to discuss and decide on actions related to conflicts.

For example, a curriculum that includes "what if" questions can enrich peacemaking abilities. Two categories of questions follow; one addresses school-specific behavior and the other addresses behavior in general.

School-Specific Questions

1. What if someone loses a notebook and you find it?
2. What if you see someone stealing from a locker?
3. What if you see a student vandalizing the building?
4. What if you suspect someone of stealing your property in school?
5. What if you catch someone cheating on a test?
6. What if you overhear students planning to hurt someone?
7. What if someone makes you quite angry in school?

General Questions

1. What if you do not want someone to sit next to you on the bus?
2. What if you are called a derogatory term?
3. What if you are with your best friend and he or she decides to break the law?
4. What if you find out that someone else is seeing your date?
5. What if someone remarks that you have been stupid?
6. What if someone gives you a compliment?
7. What if you disagree with someone who is in a position of authority?

Overall, a comprehensive social peace curriculum enables students to understand how people can treat each other in a civil and peaceful manner. They have an opportunity to develop their thinking abilities and become aware of themselves and their potential to make a difference in society. The curriculum should empower them to learn and use social skills to enrich life, address fears, and manage behavior.

Resource C: Annotated List of Programs
and Curriculum Guides for Peaceful Schools

Elementary and Middle School Grades

Conflict Resolution: An Elementary School Curriculum. Gail Sadalla, Meg Holmberg, and Jim Halligan, available from Community Board Program, 1540 Market St., Suite 490, San Francisco, CA 94102; 415/552-1250.

The activities and illustrations address the reduction of tension and hostility, ways to resolve conflicts, and communications skills. The curriculum offers a vision of how conflict resolution works in the classroom. A comprehensive bibliography and quick-reference appendices are included. Training is available. Targeted for grades K-8.

Creative Conflict Resolution: Over 200 Activities for Keeping Peace in the Classroom K-6. William J. Kreidler (1984). Scott, Foresman, Glenview, IL.

This curriculum guide focuses on improving communication skills, on developing skills to handle anger and frustration, and on teaching cooperation and tolerance of diversity. Targeted for grades K-6.

A Curriculum on Conflict Management. Uvaldo Palomares and Ben Logan. Human Development Training Institute, 7574 University Ave., La Mesa, CA 92041; 714/462-8230.

The program contains lesson guides to assist students in developing alternative, prosocial ways of dealing with conflict every time it occurs. Targeted for grades K-8.

Della the Dinosaur Talks About Violence and Anger Management. Johnson Institute, 7205 Ohms Lane, Minneapolis, MN 55439-2159; 612/831-1630 or 800/231-5165.

This group activities curriculum for grades K-6 helps children learn how to take care of themselves in stressful or violent situations, and know that they are not the cause of abuse in their homes. Targeted for grades K-6.

Fighting Fair: Dr. Martin Luther King, Jr. for Kids. Grace Contrino Abrams Peace Education Foundation, Inc., 3550 Biscayne Boulevard, Suite 400, Miami, FL 33137; 800/749-8838.

This program challenges students to resolve conflicts with skills—not fists—within the framework of Dr. Martin Luther King, Jr.'s philosophy of nonviolence. It includes an 18-minute video, a teacher's guide with reproducible student pages, and a poster of rules.

High Five Program. Center for Safe Schools and Communities, 20882 Redwood Road, Castro Valley, CA 94546; 510/247-0191.

This program consists of five steps in helping high-risk youths become healthier self-advocates through anger control and conflict management in the classroom.

Kelso's Choice. Rhinestone Press, P.O. Box 30, Winchester, OR 97495-0030; 503/672-3826.

This skill-based program has structured and sequential activities to teach conflict management to elementary children. Targeted for grades K-6.

Kids + Guns = A Deadly Equation. 1450 Northeast 2nd Ave., Room 523A, Miami, FL 33132; 305/995-1986.

This program is designed to teach young children the dangers of playing with or carrying weapons. The school-based program helps students learn to avoid weapons. Targeted for grades K-12.

Learning the Skills of Peacemaking. Childswork/Childsplay, Center for Applied Psychology, Inc., P.O. Box 1586, King of Prussia, PA 19406; 800/962-1141.

This activity guide offers teachers 56 lessons with concrete activities that allow elementary children to learn conflict resolution skills. Targeted for grades K-6.

Lion's Quest: Skills for Growing and Skills for Adolescence: K-8. Quest International, 537 Jones Road, P.O. Box 566, Granville, OH 43023-0566; 800/446-2700.

In this text, prosocial and problem-solving skills are taught with emphasis on prevention. Students are trained in accepting differences, building self-confidence, listening, expressing opinions and emotions in positive ways, resisting negative peer pressure, and being assertive. Training and videos are available. Targeted for grades K-8.

The Magic of Conflict Workshop for Young People. Judith Warner, available from Aiki Works, P.O. Box 251, Victor, NY 14564; 716/924-7302.

This curriculum is based on the work of Thomas Crum; learning-disabled students repeatedly experience conflict on a physical level and then apply the experience to nonphysical conflict.

Model Peace Education Program in New York City's Community School District 15. Eileen Jones, available from Community School District 15, 360 Smith St., Brooklyn, NY 11231.

This is a districtwide conflict resolution program for elementary and junior high students.

PATHS: Providing Alternative Thinking Strategies. Ken Dodge. Vanderbilt University, Nashville, TN 37240; 615/322-7311.

This program is designed to teach young people appropriate behavior skills and how to identify and handle their emotions. A parent training component is included.

Peace Education at Spruce Street School. Contact: Marilyn Bauer, Spruce Street School, 701 Spruce Street, Sauk City, WI 53583.

This is a schoolwide program designed to help elementary school students become aware of conflicts and intercept them before they become problems. Targeted for grades 2-5.

The Peacemaker Program. David W. Johnson and Roger T. Johnson. Cooperative Learning Center, 202 Pattee Hall, 150 Pillsbury Drive SE, Minneapolis, MN 55455-0298; 612/624-7131.

The lessons in this curriculum help students learn (a) what conflicts are, (b) how to use a six-step negotiation procedure to solve problems wisely, and (c) how to mediate classmates' conflicts. Targeted for grades 5-8.

Peer Conflict Manager Program. Susan Schultz. Equity Advocate, Ann Arbor Public Schools, 2555 S. State Street, Ann Arbor, MI 48106; 313/994-2200.

This curriculum teaches skills to manage conflicts effectively. It contains classroom lessons and parent training workshop lessons.

Project REACH. Langston Hughes Intermediate School, 11301 Ridge Heights Road, Reston, VA 22091.

This intervention curriculum contains materials and dramatic activities aimed at schools with few minority students. It has been successful in creating positive awareness of minorities by teaching human awareness skills.

Second Step: A Violence Prevention Curriculum. Committee for Children, 172 20th Avenue, Seattle, WA 98122; 800/634-4449.

The program contains lessons using puppet shows, songs, and role playing that are designed to help children avoid becoming victimizers of others by increasing their skills in empathy, impulse control, and anger management. Targeted for grades K-8.

Student Conflict Resolution. Peace Education Foundation, Inc., 2627 Biscayne Boulevard, Suite 400, Miami, FL 33137-3854; 800/749-8838.

This series of interdisciplinary curricula teaches communication, listening, critical thinking, problem-solving, decision-making, and mediation skills through puppetry, role-playing, discussion, video, and the mediation process. Both a newsletter and training are available. Targeted for grades P-9.

Students Participating Equally In Resolution (SPEIR). Contact: Neal Neto, Dayton City Schools, Roosevelt Center, 2013 West Third Street, Dayton, OH 45417; 513/262-2765.

This program trains elementary school students to use peer mediators to keep school yard disagreements from exploding into violence.

Teaching Students To Be Peacemakers. David W. Johnson and Roger T. Johnson (1991). Interaction Book Company, Edina, MN.

This program consists of curriculum with thirty 30-minute lessons that provide role-playing and other opportunities for elementary students to practice the procedures and skills involved in negotiating and mediating.

Violence Intervention Program. Durham Public Schools, P.O. Box 30002, Durham, NC 27702; 919/560-2035.

Designed to help at-risk elementary school children, the VIP program pairs children with teachers who help them with conflict mediation and resolution skills and also serve as peer counselors and tutors.

The Wonderful World of Difference and *A World of Difference.* Anti-Defamation League of B'nai B'rith, 823 United Nations Plaza, New York, NY 10017.

These programs provide a comprehensive curriculum and public campaign against prejudice. They contain a module of 20 activities for elementary school students to encourage appreciation for people of all races.

Middle and High School Grades

Anger Management and Violence Prevention: A Group Activities Manual for Middle and High School Students. Johnson Institute, 7205 Ohms Lane, Minneapolis, MN 55439-2159; 612/831-1630 or 800/231-5165.

This group activities manual helps teenagers deal with their own anger and anger expressed through violence in their homes.

Conflict Resolution: A Secondary School Curriculum. Community Board Program, 1540 Market Street, Suite 490, San Francisco, CA 94102; 415/552-1250.

Users will find everything needed, from concepts to activities, to begin teaching conflict resolution. Background sections for the instructor thoroughly explain concepts, techniques precede each chapter's activities, and a helpful bibliography with supplementary information covering special concerns and values implicit in teaching conflict resolution is provided. Targeted for grades 7-12.

Conflict Resolution Curriculum Packet. Tom and Frances Bigda-Peyton. Published by Boston-Area Educators for Social Responsibility, 11 Garden Street, Cambridge, MA 02138.

Developed by schoolteachers to teach high school students the basics of conflict resolution, this resource demonstrates how conflict resolution skills can be applied at all levels.

Dispute Resolution Curriculum in the Chicago Public Schools. Vivian Einstein-Gordan. West Publishing Company, P.O. Box 64526, 50 W. Kellogg Street, St. Paul, MN 55102-1611.

This 6-week unit introduces high school students to negotiation, mediation, and arbitration.

Fairplay. James Hills, available from FairPlay Educational Services, Inc., 48 Winona, Lawrence, KS 66046; 913/842-6313.

This conflict resolution program for students, parents, and teachers uses legal notions of due process for dealing with disputes at home and at school.

Peacemaking. Barbara Stanford (1976). Published by Bantam, New York.

A comprehensive introduction to conflict resolution by a leading educator in the field. Contains many exercises that can be used with high school students.

Project RAP (Reaching Adulthood Prepared). 380 Timothy Road, Athens, GA 30606; 706/549-1435.

Project RAP is a mentoring program for African American youth (ages 12-17) that uses church and community volunteers as role models and mentors.

Resolving Conflict Creatively. New York City Public Schools, 163 Third Avenue, #239, New York, NY 10003.

This curriculum includes units on communication, dealing with anger, intercultural relations, and mediation techniques.

Straight Talk About Risk (STAR): K-12. Contact: Gwen Fitzgerald or Susan Whitmore, Communications Division of the Center to Prevent Handgun Violence, 1225 Eye Street, N.W., Suite 1150, Washington, DC 20005; 202/289-7319.

Although STAR addresses guns specifically, the curriculum is designed to teach children life-saving behavior and conflict resolution through a variety of classroom activities that can be incorporated into existing classroom lessons. Targeted for grades K-12.

Student Support Groups. Johnson Institute, 7150 Metro Boulevard, Minneapolis, MN 55439; 800/231-5165.

This training addresses the functions and design of support groups and building groups and the strengths needed in a group leader. It focuses on individual student support systems for drug and alcohol abuse and behavior disorders.

Violence Prevention: Curriculum for Adolescents. Deborah Prothrow-Stith. Educational Development Center (EDC), 55 Chapel Street, Newton, MA 02160.
This is a 10-lesson curriculum designed to fit into high school health programs.

Violence Prevention Program. Mecklenburg County Health Department, 249 Billingsley Road, Charlotte, NC 28211; 704/336-5497.
This county program teaches conflict resolution skills and serves as a support group for youth. Targeted for grades 7-9.

Resource D: Annotated
List of Family, School, and Community Resources

ACTION Drug Prevention Program. 806 Connecticut Avenue, N.W., Suite M-606, Washington, DC 20525; 202/634-9292.
ACTION, the Federal volunteer agency, works at the local, state, and national levels to encourage and help fund the growth of youth, parent, and senior citizen groups and networks committed to helping youth remain drug free. ACTION can provide *Kids and Drugs: A Youth Leader's Handbook* and a brochure called *Idea Exchange,* which outlines 32 drug-free activities for children and teens, including ideas for speakers, publicity, community involvement, and projects.

Administration for Children, Youth, and Families. Office of Public Information and Education, P.O. Box 1182, Washington, DC 20013; 202/755-7762.
Publications from the Administration's department cover various topics, including child abuse and domestic violence. In-depth questions on child abuse are referred to the Clearinghouse on Child Abuse and Neglect Information.

American Association for Protecting Children. 9275 East Hampden Avenue, Denver, CO 80231; 303/695-0811.

This nonprofit association of organizations working to protect children from abuse and neglect provides inservice training for professionals and technical assistance for prevention programs, conducts research, maintains a database of official reports of child abuse and neglect, and provides publications on child abuse trends, research, guidelines, and standards.

American Council for Drug Education (ACDE). 204 Monroe Street, Suite 110, Rockville, MD 20852; 301/294-0600.

ACDE organizes conferences; develops media campaigns; reviews scientific findings; publishes books, a quarterly newsletter, and education kits for physicians, schools, and libraries; and produces films.

Bureau of Justice Assistance (BJA) Clearinghouse. Box 6000, Rockville, MD 29850; 800/688-4252.

This clearinghouse provides information and publications on BJA-funded anticrime and antidrug programs, including formula grants, technical assistance, training, and demonstration projects. Seven federal clearinghouses can be reached by calling 800/788-2800.

Center for Child Advocacy at Egleston Children's Hospital. 1405 Clifton Road N.E., Atlanta, GA 30322; 404/315-2268; FAX 404/315-2654.

The center has a program to serve school-based projects on child health issues, injury prevention, and parenting education. It provides free literature about safety on the playground, at home, and in the car. Also available are kits to organize community health and safety fairs at schools.

Center on Families, Communities, Schools and Children's Learning. Johns Hopkins University, 3505 N. Charles Street, Baltimore, MD 21218; 410/516-0370.

Publications from the Center include topics on parent involvement, teacher-parent connections on homework, ethnic-cultural group parenting, parent-teacher conferences, home-school collaborations, and survey questionnaires to evaluate school-family partnerships.

Centers for Disease Control (CDC). Public Inquiries, 1600 Clifton Road NE, Atlanta, GA 30333; 404/639-3286.

This organization responds to inquiries from the general public or professionals on research conducted by CDC in several areas, including injury control. If technical information is required, inquirers are referred to the appropriate CDC Center for response.

Child Welfare League of America. 440 First Street N.W., Suite 310, Washington, DC 20001; 202/638-2952.

This organization works to increase knowledge and promote understanding of child welfare problems and to improve care and services for deprived, neglected, and dependent children and their families. Materials are available on child abuse. Publications and audiovisual aids catalogs are available on request.

Clearinghouse on Child Abuse and Neglect Information. P.O. Box 1182, Washington, DC 20013; 703/821-2086.

This is a resource center for child abuse and neglect materials sponsored by the National Center on Child Abuse and Neglect. It maintains a document database that is also available on DIALOG and publishes topical bibliographies on sexual abuse, statistical data, program development, and prevention. A publications list is available.

Clearinghouse on Family Information. P.O. Box 1182, Washington, DC 20013; 703/821-2086.

They provide information services to practitioners and researchers who work to prevent family violence and assist its victims. They maintain a resource database, provide custom searches and annotated bibliographies, and offer over 100 rental audiovisual aids.

Families in Action. 1196 Henderson Mill Road, Suite 204, Atlanta, GA 30345; 404/934-6364.

This organization maintains a drug information center with more than 200,000 documents and publishes *Drug Abuse Update,* a quarterly journal containing abstracts of articles published in medical and academic journals and newspapers; $25.00 for four issues.

Family Information Center. National Agricultural Library, Room 304, 10301 Baltimore Boulevard, Beltsville, MD 20705; 301/344-3719.

The center provides information services to professionals concerned with family strengths and well-being and assists them in obtaining current literature and information. They develop resource lists and reference briefs.

Family Service America. Serverson National Information Center, 11700 West Lake Park Drive, Milwaukee, WI 53224; 414/359-2111.

An organization of family service agencies, it provides technical assistance to its 290 member agencies for the development of family-oriented policies. It publishes educational materials for practitioners, including some on topics of child abuse and family violence, and provides referrals to local agencies.

Home Instruction Programs for Preschool Youngsters (HIPPY USA). 53 West 23rd Street, New York, NY 10014; 212/645-2006.

HIPPY USA is designed for parents with limited formal schooling to provide educational enrichment for their preschool children. Support and training for the parents are given by paraprofessionals, themselves parents of young children from the communities served by the program.

Intercultural Communication Institute. 8835 Southwest Canyon Lane, Suite 238, Portland, OR 97225; 503/297-4622.

The institute is a nonprofit organization designed to foster an awareness and appreciation of cultural differences. It provides technical assistance to schools and groups on a variety of topics relating to intergroup relations.

"Just Say No" Clubs. "Just Say No" Foundation, 1777 N. California Boulevard, Suite 200, Walnut Creek, CA 94596; 800/258-2766 or 415/939-6666.

These nationwide clubs provide support and positive peer reinforcement to youngsters through workshops, seminars, newsletters, walk-a-thons, and a variety of other activities. Clubs are organized by schools, communities, and parent groups.

Kempe National Center for the Prevention and Treatment of Child Abuse and Neglect. 1205 Oneida Street, Denver, CO 80220; 303/321-3963.

This group works to improve educational, clinical, and research materials for professionals in the field; it advocates a multidisciplinary approach.

Narcotics Education, Inc. 6830 Laurel Street N.W., Washington, DC 20012; 800/548-8700—in the Washington, DC area, 202/722-6740.

This organization publishes pamphlets, books, teaching aids, posters, audiovisual aids, and prevention magazines designed for classroom use (*Winner* for preteens and *Listens* for teens).

National Committee for Prevention of Child Abuse. 332 South Michigan Avenue, Suite 950, Chicago, IL 60604; 312/663-3520.

This is an advocacy organization that offers public awareness and education programs, volunteer networks, technical assistance, and primary prevention programs. It also offers a variety of educational materials, some in Spanish.

National Crime Prevention Council. 1700 K Street N.W., Second Floor, Washington, DC 20006-3817.

This organization provides program ideas and examples for the prevention of violence and crime in the community.

National Crime Survey. Bureau of Crime Statistics, U.S. Department of Justice; 202/727-7765.

This is a data source for crime statistics.

National Criminal Justice Reference Service. National Institute of Justice, P.O. Box 6000, Rockville, MD 20850; 301/251-5500.

A central information resource on criminal justice, it provides reference services on a wide range of topics, including a behavioral database accessible to the public through DIALOG. It publishes topical bibliographies.

National Institute of Mental Health. Public Inquiries, Parklawn Building, Room 15C-05, 5600 Fishers Lane, Rockville, MD 20857; 301/443-4513.

This agency collects, stores, and disseminates scientific, technical, and other information on mental illness and health. It offers several consumer publications, some in Spanish. A publications list is available.

National Mental Health Association. 1021 Prince Street, Alexandria, VA 22314-2917; 703/684-7722 or 800/969-6642.

State mental health associations provide information and statistics on mental health and illnesses in their state, and local chapters provide information to individuals and community groups. The national office develops informational materials on all aspects of mental health and illness, including teen suicide. Some items are available in Spanish.

National Urban League. Department of Health and Social Welfare, 500 East 62nd Street, New York, NY 10021; 212/310-9238.

This group has conducted national demonstration projects in child abuse and neglect in the African American family. It answers inquiries, distributes publications, and refers to other appropriate information resources.

National Youth Gang Project. 969 East 60th Street, Chicago, IL 60637.

A cooperative effort between the National Youth Gang Suppression and Intervention Program and the U.S. Justice Department, the project provides reports on youth gangs, how cities have responded to the problem of gangs, and community mobilization.

Office of Juvenile Justice and Delinquency Prevention. Criminal Justice Department, Fox Valley Technical College, 1825 N. Bluemound Drive, P.O. Box 2277, Appleton, WI 54913-2277; 800/648-4966; FAX 414/735-4757.

This program provides literature and training on topics related to safe policy, gang and drug policy, child abuse, exploited children, juvenile delinquency, and law enforcement.

Office of Minority Health Resource Center. P.O. Box 37337, Washington, DC 20013; 800/444-6472.

This agency responds to inquiries about major health problems among minority populations, including homicide, suicide, and unintentional injury. It assists in locating materials and technical assistance through an automated resource persons network and materials database and provides information about the office's grants for innovative community health strategies developed by minority coalitions.

Parents' Resource Institute for Drug Education, Inc. (PRIDE). Woodruff Building, Suite 1002, 100 Edgewood Avenue, Atlanta, GA 30303; 800/241-9746.

This national resource and information center offers consultant services to parent groups, school personnel, and youth groups and provides a drug-use survey service. It conducts an annual conference; publishes a newsletter, a youth group handbook, and other publications; and sells and rents books, films, videos, and slide programs. Membership is $20.00.

Project SHARE. P.O. Box 30666, Bethesda, MD 20814; 800/537-3788 or 301/907-6523.

This group focuses on programmatic areas of the Family Support Administration (U.S. Department of Health and Human Services). It provides reference services designed to improve management of human services by integrating them at the delivery level. It maintains a database of documents, program descriptions, and accounts of experiences of state and local governments in planning and management. Professional materials are available on domestic violence.

TARGET. National Federation of State High School Associations, 11724 Plaza Circle, P.O. Box 20626, Kansas City, MO 64195; 816/ 464-5400.

Conducted by the National Federation of State High School Associations, an organization of interscholastic activities associations, TARGET offers workshops, training seminars, and an information bank on chemical use and prevention. It has a computerized referral service to substance abuse literature and prevention programs.

Toughlove. P.O. Box 1069, Doylestown, PA 18901; 800/333-1069 or 215/348-7090.

This national self-help group for parents, children, and communities emphasizes cooperation, personal initiative, avoidance of blame, and action. It publishes a newsletter, brochures, and books and holds workshops.

Resource E: Resource
Organizations for Teaching Peace

American Bar Association, Special Committee on Dispute Resolution, 1800 M Street, N.W., Suite 200, Washington, DC 20036; 202/331-2258.

Cambridge Ridge and Latin High School's Student Mediation Program, 459 Broadway, Cambridge, MA 02138. Contact: John Silva, 617/349-6772.

Center for Teaching Peace, 4501 Van Ness Street, N.W., Washington, DC 20016.

Center to Prevent Handgun Violence, 1225 I Street, N.W., Suite 1150, Washington, DC 20005; 202/289-7319.

Children's Creative Response to Conflict, Box 271, 523 N. Broadway, Nyack, NY 10960; 914/358-4601.

Community Board Program, 1540 Market Street, Suite 495, San Francisco, CA 94102; 414/552-1250.

Conflict Resolution Center, University of Tennessee, Knoxville, TN. Contact person: Steve Martin, 615/974-4736.

Cooperative Learning Center, University of Minnesota, Minneapolis, MN 55455; 612/624-7031.

Educators for Social Responsibility—National Office: 3 Garden Street, Cambridge, MA 02138; 617/492-1764.; New York Office: 475 Riverside Drive, Room 450, New York, NY 10115; 212/870-3318.

Ellen Raider International, 1 Millbrook Road, New Paltz, NY 12561; 914/255-5174.

Fellowship Farm, 2488 Sanatoga Road, Pottstown, PA 19464; 610/326-3008.

The Institute for Peace and Justice, 4144 Lindell Boulevard #400, St. Louis, MO 63108; 314/533-4445.

International Center for Cooperation and Conflict Resolution, Box 53, Teachers College, Columbia University, New York, NY 10027; 212/678-3402.

Iowa Peace Institute, 917 10th Avenue, Grinnell, IA 50112; 515/236-4880.

Male Health Alliance for Life Extension, 10 Sunnybrook Road, P.O. Box 1409, Raleigh, NC 27620; 919/250-4535.

National Association for Mediation in Education (NAME), University of Massachusetts at Amherst, 425 Amity Street, Amherst, MA 01002; 413/545-2462.

National Center on Fathers and Families, University of Pennsylvania, 3700 Walnut Street, Box 58, Philadelphia, PA 19104-6216; 215/686-3910.

National Coalition Building Institute International, 1835 K Street N.W., Suite 715, Washington, DC 20006; 202/785-9400; FAX 202/785-3385.

National Conference on Peacemaking and Conflict Resolution, George Mason University, 4400 University Drive, Fairfax, VA 22030; 703/993-3635.

National Council on Crime and Delinquency, 77 Maiden Lane, Fourth Floor, San Francisco, CA 94108.

National Educational Service, 1610 West Third Street, P.O. Box B, Bloomington, IN 47402.

National Institute Against Prejudice and Violence, 710 Lombard Street, Baltimore, MD 21201; 410/706-5170.

National Institute for Dispute Resolution, 1901 L Street N.W., Suite 600, Washington, DC 20036; 202/466-4764.

National School Safety Center, 4165 Thousand Oaks Boulevard, Suite 290, Westlake Village, CA 91362; 800/373-9977.

Peace Education Foundation, Inc., 2627 Biscayne Boulevard, Miami, FL 33137-3854; 305/576-5075 or 800/749-8838.

Peace Education Now, P.O. Box 4157, Gainesville, FL 32613; 904/376-0642.

Peace Grows, Inc., 475 West Market Street, Akron, OH 44304.

Project SMART, School Mediator's Alternative Resolution Team, c/o Victims Services Agency, 50 Court Street, 8th Floor, Brooklyn, NY 11201; 718/858-9070.

Resolving Conflict Creatively Program (RCCP), New York City Public Schools, 163 Third Avenue, Room 239, New York, NY 10003; 212/260-6290.

School Initiatives Program, Community Board Center for Policy and Training, 1540 Market Street, Suite 490, San Francisco, CA 94102; 415/552-1250.

School Mediation Associates, 702 Green Street #8, Cambridge, MA 02139; 617/876-6074.

Southern Poverty Law Center, 400 Washington Avenue, Montgomery, AL 36104; FAX 205/264-3121.

U.S. Department of Justice, Community Relations Service (National Office), Suite 330, 5550 Friendship Boulevard, Chevy Chase, MD 20815; 301/492-5929. Regional office: 75 Piedmont Avenue, NE, Room 900, Atlanta, GA 30303; 404/331-6883.

Resource F: Annotated List of Children's Literature for a Social Peace Curriculum

Early Elementary Grades

Theme: Friendship and Cooperation

Barker, M. (1989). *Magical hands*. Saxonville, MA: Picture Book Studio.
Four friends recognize that friendship enriches their lives.

Burningham, J. (1976). *Mr. Gumpy's motor car*. New York: Harper-Collins.
Travelers have to work together to get their car out of the mud.

Havill, J. (1993). *Jamaica and Brianna*. Boston: Houghton Mifflin.
An African American girl and an Asian American girl realize that their friendship is very special.

Heine, H. (1982). *Friends*. New York: Macmillan.
Animal friends enjoy each other when they are together and when they are separated. It provides a wonderful example of friendship.

Hoopes, L. (1990). *Wing-a-ding*. Boston: Little, Brown/Joy Street.
Friends and passersby help Jack get his toy out of the tree in which it has become stuck.

Knapp, T. (1988). *The gossamer tree: A Christmas fable*. Colorado Springs, CO: Rockrimmon Press.
Field mice, a cricket, a ladybug, a firefly, and a spider become friends during a storm. They cooperate to achieve a difficult task.

Reiser, L. (1993). *Margaret and Margarita, Margarita y Margaret*. New York: Greenwillow.

Two preschoolers who do not speak each other's language have a day of fun and enjoyment. The new friends share many special treats.

Theme: Disputes and Conflicts

Boegehold, B. (1991). *The fight.* New York: Bantam.
An accident creates a situation in which students get into a fight. The story explores what happens when students use their fists rather than their heads to try to resolve disputes.

Bunting, E. (1990). *The wall.* New York: Clarion.
This story explores both a child's and his father's emotional responses to the Vietnam Veterans Memorial Wall when they find a relative's name.

Coerr, C. (1977). *Sadako and the thousand paper cranes.* New York: G. P. Putnam.
A child's effort to understand her personal experience with the bombing of Hiroshima. It presents the effects of war on a very personal level from a child's perspective.

Gikow, L., & Weiss, E. (1993). *For every child a better world.* Racine, WI: Western/Golden.
Kermit the Frog explains that basic human needs are not available for all children. An enlightening discussion of the plight of children around the world, this book emphasizes that all of us need a clean, safe world.

Paek, M. (1988). *Aeykung's dream.* Emeryville, CA: Children's Book Press.
A young Korean girl has difficulties with her classmates because she is different. Her family helps her learn to adjust and make friends.

Theme: Peace and Harmony

Dorros, A. (1991). *Tonight is carnival.* Lima, Peru: Club de Madres Virgen del Carmen.
A whole South American village prepares for a special festival.

Foreman, M. (1985). *Cat and canary.* New York: Dial.

When threatened with a disaster, a cat has to depend on a flock of birds working together to save his life.

Oakley, G. (1983). *The church mice in action.* New York: Atheneum.
A group of mice cooperate to save their friend.

Polacco, P. (1992). *Chicken Sunday.* New York: Philomel.
Children in a community work together to earn enough money to buy a beloved friend a new hat.

Schulevitz, U. (1990). *Toddlecreek post office.* New York: Farrar Straus Giroux.
A small village in upstate New York loses its favorite meeting place.

Middle Grades

Theme: Friendship and Cooperation

Cohen, B. (1985). *The secret grove.* New York: Union of American Hebrew Congregations.
Two boys become friends even though their countries are enemies.

Dolphin, L. (1993). *Neve shalom/wahat al-salam: Oasis of peace.* New York: Scholastic.
An Arab student and a Jewish student come to understand and learn each other's culture as they develop a true friendship.

Hurwitz, J. (1990). *Class president.* New York: William Morrow.
A classroom battle teaches that all students have special talents and can work as friends to accomplish a common goal.

Lindgren, A. (1983). *Ronia, the robber's daughter.* New York: Viking.
A fantasy in which the daughter and son of two enemies become friends.

Myers, W. (1988). *Me, Mop, and the Moondance Kid.* New York: Delacorte.
Three friends who are growing up in an integrated neighborhood share special times through recreational activities.

Theme: Disputes and Conflicts

Fox, P. (1984). *One-eyed cat.* New York: Bradbury.
    This book explores the use of toys as weapons. A disobedient boy injures a cat with his air rifle and regrets his actions.

Keats, E. (1969). *Goggles.* New York: Macmillan.
    A pair of lensless motorcycle goggles are at the center of a dispute. Two boys must outsmart the neighborhood bullies.

Myers, W. (1988). *Scorpions.* New York: HarperCollins.
    Two brothers' involvement in gang activities explores in a realistic manner the conflicts and subsequent death that occur too often as a result of gang activities.

Newton, D. (1992). *Gun control: An issue for the nineties.* Hillside, NJ: Enslow.
    Arguments for and against gun control are presented.

Theme: Peace and Harmony

Durrell, A., & Sachs, M. (1990). *The big book for peace.* New York: E. P. Dutton.
    Children's authors and illustrators promote peace through poetry and stories.

Nye, N. (1992). *This same sky: A collection of poems from around the world.* New York: Four Winds.
    Words of hope and encouragement are provided by poets from around the world along with artwork, poems, and stories. The focus is on promoting harmony and doing away with strife and fighting.

Temple, L. (1993). *Dear world: How children around the world feel about the environment.* New York: Random House.
    A global perspective on people serving as caretakers of the planet. Many issues such as pollution, scarcity of resources, and protecting wildlife are addressed.

Upper Grades

Theme: Friendship and Cooperation

Hartling, P. (1988). *Crutches*. New York: Lothrop.
A boy finds a special friend in war-torn Austria.

Sirof, H. (1993). *Because she's my friend*. New York: Atheneum.
Two girls become friends and help each other overcome difficulties.

Theme: Disputes and Conflicts

Guy, R. (1979). *The disappearance*. New York: Delacorte.
Imamu leaves his home in search of a better life.

Hamilton, V. (1992). *Many thousand gone: African Americans from slavery to freedom*. New York: Knopf.
Recountings of the journey and hardships of slaves on their way to freedom.

Mahon, K. (1994). *Just one tear*. New York: Lothrop.
This is a traumatic story of the author's witnessing the fatal shooting of his father, told through diary entries.

Theme: Peace and Harmony

Carter, J. (1993). *Talking peace: A vision for the next generation*. New York: E. P. Dutton.
President Jimmy Carter's frank discussion on conflict resolution, peacemaking, and negotiations for individuals as well as nations.

Meyer, C. (1993). *White lilacs*. Orlando, FL: Harcourt Brace.
An entire African American community must relocate when a park is to be built in their neighborhood.

Resource G: Bibliography of Children's Books

Upper Grades

Adler, C. S. (1990). *Ghost brother* (pp. 160). New York: Clarion.

Cooney, C. B. (1990). *The faces on the milk carton* (pp. 144). New York: Bantam.

Grove, V. (1990). *The fastest friend in the west* (pp. 176). New York: Scholastic.

Hinton, S. E. (1967). *The outsiders* (pp. 192). New York: Viking.

Kehret, P. (1991). *Cages* (pp. 160). New York: Cobblehill.

Klass, D. (1987). *Breakway run* (pp. 176). New York: Lodestar.

Landau, E. (1991). *Weight* (pp. 160). New York: Lodestar.

Osborne, M. P. (1986). *Last one home* (pp. 160). New York: Dial.

Pershall, M. K. (1990). *You take the high road* (pp. 256). New York: Dial.

Schami, R. (1989). *A hand full of stars* (pp. 224). New York: Dutton.

Terkel, S. N. (1992). *Ethics* (pp. 160). New York: Lodestar.

Weaver-Gelzer, C. (1992). *In the time of trouble* (pp. 224). New York: E. P. Dutton.

Middle Grades

Baker, B. (1989). *Third grade is terrible* (R. Shephard, Ill., pp. 112). New York: E. P. Dutton.

Bishop, C. H. (1992). *All alone* (F. Rojanovsky, Ill., pp. 96). New York: Viking.

Clyde, R. B. (1990). *The Christmas coat* (S. Wickstrom, Ill., pp. 48). New York: Knopf.

Collura, M. E. L. (1986). *Winners* (pp. 136). New York: Dial.

Cooper, I. (1990). *Choosing sides* (pp. 224). New York: William Morrow.

Duffey, B. (1990). *The math wiz* (J. Wilson, Ill., pp. 67). New York: Viking.

Duffey, B. (1991). *The gadget war* (J. Wilson, Ill., pp. 64). Viking.

Eisenberg, L. (1991). *Happy birthday, Lexie!* (pp. 124). New York: Viking.

Herman, C. (1989). *Millie Cooper, take a chance* (H. Cogancherry, Ill., pp. 112). New York: E. P. Dutton.

Hill, E. S. (1992). *Broadway chances* (pp. 160). New York: Viking.

Johansen, H. (1991). *The duck and the owl* (K. Bhend, Ill., pp. 64). New York: E. P. Dutton.

Johnson, E. R. (1992). *A house full of strangers* (pp. 160). New York: Cobblehill.

Kinsey-Warnock, N. (1991). *The night the bells rang* (pp. 80). New York: Cobblehill.

Klein, R. (1990). *Came back to show you I could fly* (pp. 196). New York: Viking.

Klein, R. (1991). *Tearaways, stories to make you think twice* (pp. 144). New York: Viking.

Mathis, S. B. (1971). *Sidewalk story* (pp. 64). Viking.

McDonnell, C. (1990). *Friends first* (pp. 176). Viking.

Miller, M. J. (1990). *Me and my name* (pp. 121). New York: Viking.

Miller, M. J. (1992). *Upside down* (pp. 128). New York: Viking.

Moeri, L. (1979). *The girl who lives on the ferris wheel* (pp. 128). New York: E. P. Dutton.

Orgel, D. (1991). *Nobodies and somebodies* (pp. 160). New York: Viking.

Pearson, K. (1992). *Looking at the moon* (pp. 224). New York: Viking.

Phillips, L. (1983). *How do you get a horse out of the bathtub?* (J. Stevenson, Ill., pp. 80). New York: Viking.

Rabe, B. (1986). *Margaret's moves* (J. Downing, Ill., pp. 112). New York: E. P. Dutton.

Reuter, B. (1989). *Buster's world* (pp. 154). New York: E. P. Dutton.

Scholes, K. (1990). *Peace begins with you* (R. Ingpen, Ill., pp. 40). Boston: Sierra Club/Little, Brown.

Singer, M. (1990). *Twenty ways to lose your best friend* (J. Lindberg, Ill., pp. 128). New York: HarperCollins.

Smith, D. B. (1983). *The first hard times* (pp. 144). New York: Viking.

Wittman, S. (n.d.). *Jessie's wishes* (E. A. McCully, Ill., pp. 112). New York: Scholastic.

Preschool and Primary

Impey, R., & Knox, J. (1990). *No-name dog* (pp. 64). New York: E. P. Dutton.

Saunders, S., & Bjorkman, S. (1992). *Tyrone goes to school* (pp. 64). New York: E. P. Dutton.

Stapler, S. (1990). *Cordelia, dance!* (pp. 32). New York: Dial.

Wahl, J. (1991). *Mrs. Owl and Mr. Pig* (pp. 32). New York: Lodestar.

Warburton, N. (1992). *Mr. Tite's belongings* (pp. 32). New York: Viking.

Wells, R. (1978). *Stanley and Rhoda* (pp. 40). New York: Dial.

Wells, R. (1981). *Timothy goes to school* (pp. 32). New York: Dial.

Wells, R. (1989). *Max's chocolate chicken* (pp. 32). New York: Dial.

Additional Children's Books

Ayer, E. (1992). *Boris Yeltsin: Man of the people* (pp. 144). New York: Dillon.

Ballard, R. (1993). *Gracie* (unpaged). New York: Greenwillow.

Banish, R. (1992). *A forever family* (pp. 44). New York: HarperCollins.

Bauman, K. (1993). *The hungry one* (pp. 32) (S. Eidrigevicius, Ill., N. Lewis, Trans.). New York: North-South.

Birdseye, T. (1993). *Just call me stupid* (pp. 128). New York: Scholastic.

Caruana, C. (1992). *The abortion debate* (pp. 64). Brookfield, CT: Millbrook.

Cavan, S. (1993). *Thurgood Marshall and equal rights* (pp. 32). Brookfield, CT: Millbrook.

Chalofsky, M., Finland, G., & Wallace, J. (1992). *Changing places: A kid's view of shelter living* (I. Klass, Ill., pp. 61). Mt. Rainier, MD: Gryphon House.

Chang, M., & Chang, R. (1990). *In the eyes of war* (pp. 197). New York: McElderry.

Charles, V. (1993). *The crane girl* (unpaged). New York: Orchard.

Charters, J., & Foreman, M. (1961). *The general* (unpaged). New York: E. P. Dutton.

Cottonwood, J. (1992). *Danny ain't* (pp. 288). New York: Scholastic.

Cwiklik, R. (1993). *Bill Clinton: Our 42nd president* (pp. 48). Brookfield, CT: Millbrook.

Danziger, P. (1982). *The divorce express* (pp.144). New York: Delacorte.

Davey, T. (1984). *Waiting for May* (pp. 48). New York: Doubleday.

Duden, J. (1992). *1992 timelines annuals* (pp. 48). New York: Crestwood.

Durrell, A., & Sachs, M. (1990). *The big book of peace* (pp. 120). New York: E. P. Dutton.

Duvoisin, R. A. (1961). *The happy hunter* (pp. 32). New York: Lothrop.

Estes, E. (1944). *The hundred dresses* (pp. 78). New York: Scholastic.

Fitzhugh, L., & Scoppetone, S. (1969). *Bang, bang, you're dead* (pp. 32). New York: HarperCollins.

Ford, M. (1992). *100 questions and answers about AIDS* (pp. 208). New York: New Discovery.

Foreman, M. (1972). *Moose* (pp. 32). New York: Pantheon.

Garland, S. (1993). *The lotus seed* (T. Kiuchi, Ill., pp. 32). New York: Harcourt Brace.

Geography Department. (1993). *Belarus* (pp. 56). Minneapolis, MN: Lerner.

Gordon, S. (1990). *The middle of somewhere: A story of South Africa* (pp. 154). New York: Orchard.

Greene, C. C. (1969). *A girl called Al* (pp. 127). New York: Dell.

Hader, B. H. (1960). *Mister Billy's gun* (unpaged). New York: Macmillan.

Hahn, M. (1988). *December stillness* (pp. 92). New York: Clarion.

Hamilton, V. (1990). *Cousins* (pp. 125). New York: Philomel.

Heide, F. P., & Gilliland, J. H. (1992). *Sami and the time of the troubles* (pp. 32). New York: Clarion.

Ho, M. (1991). *The clay marble* (pp. 163). New York: Farrar Straus Giroux.

Hopkins, L. B. (Ed.). (1992). *Through our eyes* (J. Dunn, Ill., pp. 32). Boston: Little, Brown.

Hughes, L. (1992). *Nelson Mandela: Voice of freedom* (pp. 144). New York: Dillon.

Ikeda, D. (1992). *Over the deep blue sea* (B. Wildsmith, Ill., pp. 32). New York: Knopf.

Joosee, B. (1992). *Nobody's cat* (M. Sewall, Ill., pp. 32). New York: HarperCollins.

Lacoe, A. (1992). *Just not the same* (P. Estrada, Ill., pp. 32). Boston: Houghton Mifflin.

Leaf, Munro. (1936). *The story of Ferdinand the bull* (R. Lawson, Ill., unpaged). New York: Viking.

Leigh, N. (1993). *Learning to swim in Swaziland* (pp. 48). New York: Scholastic.

Levine, E. (1989). *I hate English* (S. Bjorkman, Ill., pp. 32). New York: Scholastic.

Levine, E. (1993). *Freedom's children* (pp. 167). New York: G. P. Putnam.

Little, J. (1992). *Revenge of the small small* (J. Wilson, Ill., pp. 32). New York: Viking.

Lobel, N. (1967). *Potatoes, potatoes* (pp. 40). New York: Greenwillow.

Naidoo, B. (1989). *Chain of fire* (E. Velasquez, Ill., pp. 245). New York: Lippincott.

Namioka, L. (1992). *Yang the youngest and his terrible ear* (pp. 134). Boston: Little, Brown.

Nelson, V. (1993). *Mayfield crossing* (L. Jenkins, Ill., pp. 88). New York: Putnam.

Nichols, K. (1992). *Sarah* (F. Nichols, Ill., pp. 22). Topeka, KS: Lone Tree.

Park, B. (1981). *Don't make me smile* (pp. 114). New York: Avon.

Peet, B. (1963). *The pinkish, purplish, bluish egg* (pp. 46). Boston: Houghton Mifflin.

Peterson, J. (1970). *Mean Max* (pp. 48). New York: Scholastic.

Ricciuti, E. (1993). *War in Yugoslavia* (pp. 64). New York: Millbrook.

Rofes, E. E. (Ed.). (1982). *The kid's book of divorce* (pp. 44). New York: Vintage.

Russo, M. (1993). *Trade-in mother* (pp. 32). New York: Greenwillow.

Salak, J. (1993). *The Los Angeles riots* (pp. 64). Brookfield, CT: Millbrook.

Schilling, S., & Swain, J. (1989). *My name is Jonathan and I have AIDS* (pp. 49). East Haven, CT: Prickly Pair.

Seymour, T. (1993). *Pole dog* (D. Soman, Ill., pp. 32). New York: Orchard.

Seymour-Jones, C. (1992). *Homelessness* (pp. 48). New York: New Discovery.

Seymour-Jones, C. (1992). *Refugees* (pp. 48). New York: New Discovery.

Sharmat, M. W. (1975). *Walter the wolf* (K. Oechsli, Ill., pp. 32). New York: Holiday House.

Shles, L. (1992). *Scooter's tail of terror* (pp. 80). Rolling Hills Estates, CA: Jalmar.

Smith, D. (1993). *Best girl* (pp. 144). New York: Viking Children's Books.

Stowe, C. (1992). *Dear mom, in Ohio for a year* (pp. 180). New York: Scholastic.

Taylor, C. (1992). *The house that crack built* (pp. 40). San Francisco: Chronical.

Thiel, E. (1992). *The polka dot horse* (T. Milne, Ill., unpaged). New York: Simon & Schuster.

Thompson, C. (1993). *Pictures of home* (pp. 32). New York: Green Tiger.

Viorst, J. (1972). *Alexander and the terrible, horrible, no good, very bad day* (R. Cruz, Ill., pp. 32). Riverside, NJ: Atheneum.

Walter, M. P. (1990). *Two and too much* (P. Cummings, Ill., pp. 32). New York: Bradbury.

Whelan, G. (1992). *Bringing the farmhouse home* (J. Rowland, Ill.). New York: Simon & Schuster.

Wiesner, W. (1969). *Tops*. New York: Viking.

Wild, M. (1993). *Space travellers* (G. Rogers, Ill.). New York: Scholastic.

Williams, K. L. (1991). *When Africa was home* (Floyd Cooper, Ill., pp. 32). New York: Orchard.

Wondriska, W. (1964). *The tomato patch.* Cambridge, MA: Holt.

Wood, D. (1992). *Old turtle* (C. Chee, Ill.). Duluth, MN: Pfeifer-Hamilton.

Yolen, J. (1993). *Jane Yolen's songs of summer* (C. Moore, Ill., pp. 32). Honesdale, PA: Boyds Mills.

Yolen, J. (1993). *Lullaby songbook* (C. Mibolsycok, Ill., pp. 32). Niles, IL: Harcourt Brace.

Resource H: Professional Literature Related to Discipline and Classroom Management

Baron, E. (1992). *Discipline strategies for teachers* (PDK Fastback 344). Bloomington, IN: Phi Delta Kappa Educational Foundation.

Bluestein, J. (1988). *21st century discipline—Teaching student responsibility and self-control.* Albuquerque, NM: Instructor Books, Edgell Communications, Inc.

Borba, M. (1989). *Esteem builders: A K-8 self-esteem curriculum for improving student achievement, behavior, and school climate.* Millwood, NY: Kraus Curriculum.

Burden, P. R. (1995). *Classroom management and discipline: Methods to facilitate cooperation and instruction.* New York: Longman.

Charles, C. (1992). *Building classroom discipline* (4th ed.). New York: Longman.

Cohen, J., & Fish, M. (1993). *Handbook of school-based interventions: Resolving student problems and promoting healthy educational environments* (Jossey-Bass Social and Behavioral Science Series). San Francisco: Jossey-Bass.

Collis, M., & Dalton, J. (1990). *Becoming responsible learners—Strategies for positive classroom management.* Portsmouth, NH: Heinemann.

DeBruyn, R., & Larson, J. (1984). *You can handle them all: A discipline model for handling over one hundred different misbehaviors at school and at home.* Manhattan, KS: The Master Teacher.

Dreikurs, R., & Cassel, P. (1974). *Discipline without tears* (2nd ed.). New York: Hawthorn.

Duke, D. (1980). *Managing student behavior problems.* New York: Teachers College Press.

Emmer, E., Evertson, C., Clements, B., & Worsham, M. (1994). *Classroom Management for secondary teachers.* Boston: Allyn & Bacon.

ERIC Clearinghouse on Elementary and Early Childhood Education. (1990). *Positive discipline.* (ERIC Document Reproduction Service No. ED 327 271)

Evertson, C., Clements, B., Sanford, J., & Worsham, M. (1994). *Classroom management for elementary teachers* (3rd ed.). Englewood Cliffs, NJ: Prentice Hall.

Gartrell, D. (1994). *A guidance approach to discipline.* Albany, NY: Delmar.

Ginott, H. (1972). *Teacher and child: A book for parents and teachers.* New York: Macmillan.

Glasser, W. (1992). *The quality school: Managing students without coercion* (2nd ed.). New York: Harper-Perennial.

Haw, K. F. (1991). Interactions of gender and race—a problem for teachers? A review of the emerging literature. *Educational Research 33*(1), 12-21.

Honig, A., & Wittmer, D. (1991). *Helping children become more prosocial: Tips for teachers.* (ERIC Document Reproduction Service No. ED 343 693)

Irvine, J. (1990). *Black students and school failure: Policies, practices, and prescriptions.* New York: Greenwood.

Jones, F. (1987). *Positive classroom discipline.* New York: McGraw-Hill.

Katz, N. H., & Lawyer, J. W. (1994). *Resolving conflict successfully: Needed knowledge and skills.* Thousand Oaks, CA: Corwin.

Knight, M., Graham, T., Miksza, S., Juliano, R., & Tonnies, P. (1982). *Teaching children to love themselves—A handbook for parents and teachers of young children.* Englewood Cliffs, NJ: Prentice Hall.

Kounin, J. (1970). *Discipline and group management in classrooms.* New York: Holt, Rinehart & Winston.

Medland, M. (1990). *Self-management strategies: Theory, curriculum, and teaching procedures.* New York: Praeger.

Riley, K. (1991). *Street gangs and the schools: A blueprint for intervention* (Fastback #321). Bloomington, IN: Phi Delta Kappa.

Ryan, K. (1992). Conclusion: Rules for riding the roller coaster. In K. Ryan (Ed.), *The roller coaster year: Essays by and for beginning teachers* (pp. 247-259). New York: Harper Collins.

Schell, L., & Burden, P. (1992). *Countdown to the first day of school: A 60-day get ready checklist for first-time teachers, teacher transfers, student transfers, teacher mentors, induction-program administrators, teacher educators* (NEA Checklist Series). (ERIC Document Reproduction Service No. ED 350 115)

Swick, K. (1987). *Student stress: A classroom management system.* Washington, DC: National Education Association.

Trueba, H.T. (Ed.). (1987). *Success or failure: Learning and the language minority student.* Cambridge, MA: Newbury House.

Weinstein, C., & Mignano, A. (1993). *Elementary classroom management: Lessons from research and practice.* New York: McGraw-Hill.

Wayson, W., DeVoss, G., Kaeser, S., Lasley, T., Pinnell, G., & Phi Delta Kappa Commission on Discipline. (1982). *Handbook for developing schools with good discipline.* Bloomington, IN: Phi Delta Kappa.

Wilson, E., Alexander, J., Spann, B., Ryan, C., La Brecque, R., & Putnam, J. (1993). How do you rate as a classroom manager? *Instructor, 103*(1), 30-37.

Wolfgang, C., & Glickman, C. (1986). *Solving discipline problems: Strategies for classroom teachers* (2nd ed.). Boston: Allyn & Bacon.

Wynne, E., & Ryan, K. (1993). *Reclaiming our schools: A handbook on teaching character, academics, and discipline.* New York: Merrill.

References

American Psychological Association Commission on Violence and Youth. (1993). *Violence and youth: Psychology's response* (Vol. 1). New York: Author.

American Psychological Association Commission on Violence and Youth. (1993). *Violence and youth: Psychology's response* (Vol. 2). New York: Author.

Armstrong, T. (1994). *Multiple intelligences in the classroom.* Alexandria, VA: Association for Supervision and Curriculum Development.

Association for Supervision and Curriculum Development. (1994, September). Breaking the lockstep. *Update, 36*(7), 1.

Baker, D. P., & Stevenson, D. L. (1986). Mothers' strategies for children's school achievement: Managing the transition to high school. *Sociology of education, 59,* 156-166.

Banks, J. A. (1992). Dimensions of multicultural education. *Kappa Delta Pi Record, 29*(1), 12.

Beane, J. A., & Lipka, R. P. (1986). *Self-concept, self-esteem and the curriculum.* New York: Teachers College Press.

Bey, T. M. (1986). Complete procedural record: Helping beginning teachers set professional goals. *The Clearing House, 9*(8), 366-368.

Brekelmans, M., Levy, J., & Rodriguez, R. (1993). A typology of teacher communication style. In T. Wubbels & J. Levy (Eds.), *Do you know what you look like? Interpersonal relationships in education* (pp. 46-55). Washington, DC: Falmer.

Burke, R. R. (1995). *Communicating with students in schools* (3rd ed.). Lanham, MD: University Press of America.

Caine, R. N., & Caine, G. (1991). *Making connections: Teaching and the human brain.* Alexandria, VA: Association for Supervision and Curriculum Development.

California State Department of Education. (1989). *Safe schools: A planning guide for action.* Sacramento, CA: Author.

Carlsson-Paige, N., & Levin, D. E. (1992). Making peace in violent times: A constructivist approach to conflict resolution. *Young Children, 48*(1), 4-13.

Center for the Study of Social Policy. (1993). *Kids' count data book.* Washington, DC: Author.

Charney, R. S. (1991). *Teaching children to care: Management in the responsive classroom.* Greenfield, MA: Northeast Foundation for Children.

Cochran-Smith, M., & Lytle, S. L. (1993). *Inside/outside: Teacher research and knowledge.* New York: Teachers College Press.

Comer, J. P. (1980). *School power: Implications of an intervention project.* New York: Free Press.

Cooper, P. J. (1988). *Speech communication for the classroom teacher* (3rd ed.). Scottsdale, AZ: Gorsuch Scarisbrick.

Costen, B. M. (1994, August). *Conflict resolution.* Atlanta, GA: Department of Corrections Workshop.

Crowe, T. D. (1994). *Habitual juvenile offenders: Guidelines for citizen action and public responses* (Contract No. OJP-94-C-001). Appleton, WI: Fox Valley Technical College, Office of Juvenile Justice and Delinquency Prevention.

Cueto, S., Bosworth, K., & Sailes, J. (1993, April). *Promoting peace: Integrating curricula to deal with violence.* Paper presented at the annual meeting of the American Educational Research Association, Atlanta, GA.

Curwin, R. L., & Mendler, A. N. (1988). *Discipline with dignity.* Alexandria, VA: Association for Supervision and Curriculum Development.

Deal, T. E., & Peterson, K. D. (1991). *The principal's role in shaping school culture.* Washington, DC: U.S. Department of Education.

DeKalb County Government and Emory-Egleston Center for Child Advocacy. (1994). *Peacework: Bring us together in DeKalb* (Violence Prevention Framework). DeKalb County, GA: Author.

Doll, R. C. (1989). *Curriculum improvement: Decision making and process* (7th ed.). Boston: Allyn & Bacon.

Drew, N. (1987). *Learning the skills of peacemaking: An activity guide for elementary-age children on communicating, cooperating, resolving conflict.* Rolling Hills Estates, CA: Jalmar.

Duttweiler, P. C., & Hord, S. M. (1987). *Dimensions of effective leadership.* Austin, TX: Southwest Educational Development Laboratory.

Egleston Children's Hospital Center for Child Advocacy. (1992). *Family routines* (flyer). (Available from author, 1405 Clifton Road N.E., Atlanta, GA 03022, 404/325-6000)

Elam, S. M., Rose, L. C., & Gallup, A. M. (1994). The 26th Annual Phi Delta Kappa Gallup poll of the public's attitudes toward the public schools. *Phi Delta Kappan 76*(1), 41-56.

Elias, M. J., & Clabby, J. F. (1992). *Building social problem-solving skills.* San Francisco: Jossey-Bass.

Epstein, J. L. (1992). School and family partnerships. In M. Alkin (Ed.), *Encyclopedia of Educational Research* (6th ed., pp. 1139-1151). New York: Macmillan.

Gantt, C. (1992). Unite: Understanding needs: Integrating team efforts/services and collaborating agencies and the school. In L. M. Tomlinson (Ed.), *The imperative educational network: Parents, teachers, and concerned individuals* (Vol. 4, pp. 62-81). Athens: University of Georgia Press.

Gardner, H. (1983). *Frames of mind.* New York: Basic Books.

Gardner, H., & Hatch, T. (1989). Multiple intelligences go to school. *Educational Researcher, 18*(8), 4-10.

Gay, G. (1994). *At the essence of learning: Multicultural education.* West Lafayette, IN: Kappa Delta Pi.

George, P. S., Stevenson, C., Thomason, J., & Beane, J. (1992). *The middle school—and beyond.* Alexandria, VA: Association for Supervision and Curriculum Development.

Glatthorn, A. A. (1987). *Curriculum leadership.* Glenview, IL: Scott, Foresman.

Gold, Y., & Roth, R. A. (1993). *Teachers managing stress and preventing burnout: The professional health solution.* Bristol, PA: Falmer.

Hamilton, D., & Osborne, S. (1994). Overcoming barriers to parent involvement in public schools. *Kappa Delta Pi Record, 30*(4), 148-152.

Hass, G. (1987). *Curriculum planning: A new approach* (7th ed.). Boston: Allyn & Bacon.

Houston, R., & Grubaugh, S. (1989). Language for preventing and defusing violence in the classroom. *Urban Education, 24* (1), 23-37.

Howe, Q., Jr. (1991). *Under running laughter: Notes from a renegade classroom.* New York: Free Press.

Kadel, S., & Follman, J. (1993). *Reducing school violence.* Atlanta, GA: SouthEastern Regional Vision for Education.

Kohl, H. R. (1967). *Teaching the unteachable: The story of an experiment in children's writing.* New York: New York Review.

Kozol, J. (1991). *Savage inequalities: Children in America's schools.* New York: Crown.

Kreidler, W. J. (1984). *Creative conflict resolution.* Glenview, IL: Scott, Foresman.

Leake, D. (1993, April 19). Ensuring racial, cultural harmony in the school. *NASSP Bulletin, 77,* 33-36.

Lichtenstein, R., Schonfeld, D. J., & Kline, M. (1994). School crisis response: Expecting the unexpected. *Educational Leadership, 52*(3), 79-83.

Love, A., & Roderick, J. (1971). Teacher nonverbal communication: The development and field testing of an awareness unit. *Theory Into Practice, 10,* 295-299.

Marzano, R. J., Brandt, R. S., Hughes, C. S., Jones, B. F., Presseisen, B. Z., Rankin, S. C., & Suhor, C. (1988). *Dimensions of thinking: A framework for curriculum and instruction.* Alexandria, VA: Association for Supervision and Curriculum Development.

McCarthy, C. (1992). Why we must teach peace. *Educational Leadership, 50*(1), 6-9.

McClellan, M. (1994). Why blame schools? *Research Bulletin, 12.* Bloomington, IN: Phi Delta Kappa Center for Evaluation, Development, and Research.

McConaghy, T. (1986). Peace education: A controversial issue? *Phi Delta Kappan, 68*(4), 248-249.

Messing, J. K. (1993). Mediation: An intervention strategy for counselors. *Journal of Counseling and Development, 72,* 67-72.

Metropolitan Life Survey of the American Teacher. (1993). *Violence in America's public schools.* New York: Metropolitan Life Insurance Company.

Moore, K. D. (1989). *Classroom teaching skills: A primer.* New York: Random House.

National Association of Social Workers. (1994). *100 Ways You Can Stop Violence.* Washington, DC: Author.

National Center for Injury Prevention and Control. (1993). *The prevention of youth violence: A framework for community action.* Atlanta, GA: Centers for Disease Control and Prevention.

National Research Council. (1993). *Understanding and preventing violence.* Washington, DC: National Academy Press.

Nieto, S. (1992). *Affirming diversity: The sociopolitical context of multicultural education.* White Plains, NY: Longman.

Office of Juvenile Justice and Delinquency Prevention. (1993). *Habitual juvenile offenders: Guidelines for social services* (Contract No. 89-JS-CX-K001). McLean, VA: U.S. Department of Justice, Public Administration Service.

Ordovensky, P. (1993). Facing up to violence. *Executive Educator, 15*(2), 22-25.

Paley, V. G. (1979). *White teacher.* Cambridge, MA: Harvard University Press.

Parke, R. D., & Ladd, G. W. (Eds.). (1992). *Family-peer relationships: Modes of linkage.* Hillsdale, NJ: Erlbaum.

Pelfrey, W. V. (1993). *Explanations of delinquency: Fact and fiction* (Contract No. 89-JS-CX-K001). McLean, VA: U.S. Department of Justice, Office of Juvenile Justice Programs.

Purkey, W. W., & Novak, J. (1984). *Inviting school success: A self-concept approach to teachers and learning.* Belmont, CA: Wadsworth.

Rapp, J. A., Carrington, F., & Nicholson, G. (1992). *School crime and violence: Victim's rights.* Malibu, CA: National School Safety Center.

Rich, J. M. (1993). Education and family values. *The Educational Forum, 57*(2), 162-167.

Richardson, R. C., & Evans, E. D. (1993). Empowering teachers to halt corporal punishment. *Kappa Delta Pi Record, 29*(2), 39-42.

San Diego City Schools. (1995). *Police Services Department Operations Manual* (2nd ed.). (Available from San Diego City Schools Police Department, 4100 Normal Street, San Diego, CA, 92103-2682)

Sarason, S. B. (1993). *The case for change: Rethinking the preparation of educators.* San Francisco: Jossey-Bass.

Schmuck, R. A., & Runkel, P. J. (1985). *The handbook of organization development in schools* (3rd ed.). Prospect Heights, IL: Waveland.

School, B., & Cooper, A. (1986). Reflective thinking. *Academic Therapy, 21*(4), 441-446.

Schubert, W. H. (1986). *Curriculum: Perspective, paradigm, and possibility.* New York: Macmillan.

Serious Habitual Offender Comprehensive Action Program. (1994). *Habitual juvenile offenders: Guidelines for schools* (Contract No.

OJP-94-C-001). Appleton, WI: Fox Valley Technical College, Office of Juvenile Justice and Delinquency Prevention.

Sleeter, C. E., & Grant, C. A. (1988). *Making choices for multicultural education.* Columbus, OH: Merrill.

Squires, D. (1980). *Characteristics of effective schools: The importance of school processes.* Philadelphia: Research for Better Schools, Inc. (ERIC Document Reproduction Service No. ED 197 468)

Stomfay-Stitz, A. M. (1994, April). *Peace education for children: Historical perspectives.* Paper presented at the annual meeting of the American Educational Research Association, New Orleans, LA.

Sweeney, J. T. (1983, October). *Managerial skills and educational productivity.* Paper presented at the Southwest Educational Development Laboratory Symposium on Educational Productivity, Austin, TX.

Tennessee Education Association and Appalachia Educational Laboratory. (1993). *Reducing school violence: Schools teaching peace.* Nashville, TN: Author.

Thomson, B. J. (1993). *Words can hurt you: Beginning a program of anti-bias education.* Menlo Park, CA: Addison-Wesley.

Tomlinson, L. M. (Ed.). (1992). *The imperative educational network: Parents, teachers, and concerned individuals: Vol. 4.* Athens: University of Georgia Press.

U.S. Department of Education. (1986). *What works: Research about teaching and learning.* Washington, DC: Author.

U.S. Department of Education. (1988, June). Improving student discipline. *Research in Brief.* Washington, DC: Author.

U.S. Department of Education. (1990). *Learning to live drug free: A curriculum model for prevention.* Washington, DC: Author.

U.S. Department of Education. (1991). *America 2000: An education strategy.* Washington, DC: Author.

U.S. Department of Education. (1993). *Reaching the goals, goal 6: Safe, disciplined, and drug-free schools.* Washington, DC: Author.

Useem, E. L. (1990, April). *Social class and ability group placement in mathematics in the transition to seventh grade: The role of parent involvement.* Paper presented at the annual meeting of the American Educational Research Association, Boston, MA.

Wayson, W., Devoss, G., Kaeser, S., Lasley, T., Pinnell, G., & Phi Delta Kappa Commission on Discipline. (1982). *Handbook for developing schools with good discipline.* Bloomington, IN: Phi Delta Kappa.

Index

ACTION Drug Prevention Program, 131

Administration for Children, Youth, and Families, 132

Aggression as learned response, vii

American Association for Protecting Children, 132

American Bar Association, Special Committee on Dispute Resolution, 138

American Council for Drug Education (ACDE), 132

American Psychological Association Commission on Violence and Youth, 2, 4, 101

Anger management techniques, teaching, 37

Antisocial behavior as learned response, vii

Armstrong, T., 72, 73, 81

Association for Supervision and Curriculum Development, 70

Baker, D. P., 85

Banks, J. A., 63

Beane, J., 71

Beane, J. A., 56

Bey, T. M., 57, 61

Bodily-kinesthetic intelligence, 73

Bosworth, K., 2

Brandt, R. S., 57

Brekelmans, M., 48

Bureau of Justice Assistance (BJA) Clearinghouse, 132

Burke, R. R., 48

Caine, G., 38

Caine, R. N., 38

California State Department of Education, 21

Cambridge Ridge and Latin High School's Student Mediation Program, 138

Carlsson-Paige, N., 44, 77

Carrington, F., 30

Center for Child Advocacy at Egleston Children's Hospital, 132
Center for Teaching Peace, 138
Center for the Study of Social Policy, 101
Center on Families, Communities, Schools and Children's Learning, 133
Centers for Disease Control (CDC), 133
Center to Prevent Handgun Violence, 138
Charney, R. S., 64
Children's Creative Response to Conflict, 138
Child Welfare League of America, 133
Clabby, J. F., 78
Classroom management/discipline techniques:
　academic achievement and, 29
　appropriateness of, 29
　good conduct and, 29
　need for continual renewal of, 28
　obedience approach, 28-29
　responsibility approach, 29
　zero-tolerance approach, 29, 43
Clearinghouse on Child Abuse and Neglect Information, 133
Clearinghouse on Family Information, 133
Closed-circuit television in schools, 3
Cochran-Smith, M., 69
Comer, J. P., 83
Communication:
　among school personnel, 43-44
　as peacemaking behavior, 58
　forms of, 36-43
　parent-child, 83-85
　techniques, 84-85
　See also specific forms of communication
Communication, inclusive:
　clarification and, 35
　definition of, 34
　encouragement and, 35
　negotiation and, 35
　power sharing and, 35
　reflection and, 35

Communication, negative, changing, 44-46
Communication styles:
　definition of, 47
　effective listening and, 48
　listening and, 47-48
　productive activity and, 47
　teacher, 48
　unproductive activity and, 47
Community Board Program, 138
Conflict, school, causes of, 27-28
Conflict prevention strategies, 77-78
Conflict resolution:
　as peacemaking behavior, 58
　See also Conflict resolution management; Conflict resolution skills
Conflict Resolution Center, University of Tennessee, Knoxville, 138
Conflict resolution management:
　deterring violence with, 105
　necessity of teaching, 105
Conflict resolution skills, 80
　conflict and lack of, 27
　learning, ix
Cooper, A., 38
Cooper, P. J., 40, 47, 48
Cooperation:
　as peacemaking behavior, 58
　in peaceable classrooms, 25
Cooperative Learning Center, University of Minnesota, 138
Costen, B. M., 77
Crime, juvenile, 105-106
　information, 106
　peak ages for, 105
　school administrators denying, 109
　school detectives and, 106
　See also Delinquency
Crisis management plans, 21, 109
Crowe, T. D., 108
Cueto, S., 2
Cultural communication, 36
　ethnic identity and, 42
　identity and, 42, 43
　in school, 42
　kinship and, 42

Curricular approaches, 56
Curriculum, social, 54-67
    administrative support and, 66
    children's literature for, 140-145
    communication skills activities
        in, 118
    content areas in, 121-124
    cooperative activities in, 118
    design of, 120
    environmental learning
        activities in, 118
    for middle and high school,
        120-125
    for young children, 117
    hidden curriculum and, 58-60
    moral/ethical activities in, 119
    peacemaking skills and, 124-125
    problem solving, 120-121
    revising, 56-58, 65-66
    social peace and, 64
    teacher ownership and, 66
Curwin, R. L., 29

Deal, T. E., 10
DeKalb County Government and
    Emory-Egleston Center for
    Child Advocacy, 110
Delinquency, theories for causes of,
    106-108. *See also* Crime,
    juvenile
Destructive violence, 3, 23
    forms of, 4
Devoss, G., 44
Doll, R. C., 56
Drew, N., 26, 27, 29, 80
Duttweiler, P. C., 7

Educational policy change for
    peaceable schools, 5-6
    approaches to, 9-11
    free market economic approach
        to, 10
    human resource approach to, 10
    political approach to, 10
    school culture/ethos approach
        to, 10
    structural approach to, 10
Educational process:
    infusing peace throughout, x

integration of peaceable
    concepts in, 2
integration of peaceable
    practices in, 2
integration of peaceable skills
    in, 2
Educators for Social Responsibility,
    138
Effective schools:
    cohesiveness in, 22
    communication of expectations
        in, 22
    esprit in, 23
    goal orientation in, 23
    leadership in, 23
    orderly environment and, 22
    safe environment and, 22
Egleston Children's Hospital, 98
Elam, S. M., 91
Elias, M. J., 78
Ellen Raider International, 138
Emotional communication, 36-37
    anger and, 37
    positive aspects of, 37
    verbal abuse and, 37
Emotional violence, 3, 23
    forms of, 4
Epstein, J. L., 85, 103
Evans, E. D., 90

Families in Action, 134
Family education, 86-87
    child development/learning
        education and, 87
    home visits and, 87
Family Information Center, 134
Family routines, 98
Family-school-community action
    plan for peace:
    changing values/attitudes and,
        114
    initial ideas for, 109
    juvenile justice system and, 113
    school-community involvement
        and, 110
    school enrichment activities
        and, 111
    school-neighborhood
        improvement and, 110-111

school policies and, 114
services for parents and, 111-112
suggested strategies for, 110-114
youth employment and, 112
youth services and, 112-113
Family-school-community
    partnerships:
    building, 101-115
    school-community social
        services and, 102-103
    types of, 103-104
Family-school-community
    peacebuilding groups, 110
Family-school involvement, 85-86
    activities, 97
    barriers to, 85-86
    communication barriers to, 86
    emotional barriers to, 86
    family education and, 86-87
    instilling values and, 89-91
    parent-child communication
        activities and, 83-85
    parent-friendly school support
        and, 91-92
    parent-teacher conferences and,
        93-95
    parent workshops and, 87-88
    physical barriers to, 86
    social barriers to, 86
Family Service America, 134
Fellowship Farm, 138
Follman, J., 19, 20, 21
Fourth Street Elementary School
    (Athens, GA), collaborative
    school-community social
    services in, 102

Gallup, A. M., 91
Gantt, C., 102
Gardner, H., 72
Gay, G., 30, 42
George, P. S., 71
Glatthorn, A. A., 58
Gold, Y., 12
Grant, C. A., 62
Graubaugh, S., 80

Hamilton, D., 86
Hass, G., 67

Hatch, T., 72
Home Instruction Programs for
    Preschool Youngsters
    (HIPPY USA), 134
Hord, S. M., 7
Houston, R., 80
Howe, Q., Jr., 59
Hughes, C. S., 57

ID badges in schools, 3
Institute for Peace and Justice, The,
    138
Instruction:
    innovative, 68
    lock-step method of, 70
    See also Instruction, differenti-
        ated approaches to
Instruction, differentiated ap-
    proaches to:
    contracts, 71
    cooperative learning, 70-71
    direct instruction, 71
    electronic learning, 71
    learning centers, 70
    mastery learning, 70
    self-directed projects, 71
    service learning, 71
Intellectual communication, 36
    critical thinking in, 38
    reflective learning in, 38
    reflective thinking checklist
        and, 38-39
    student activities to stimulate,
        38-39
    verbal analogy and, 38
    verbal rehearsal and, 38
    visual imagery and, 38
Intellectual functioning patterns,
    73. See also specific types of in-
    telligence
Intercultural Communication Insti-
    tute, 134
International Center for
    Cooperation and Conflict
    Resolution, 139
Interpersonal communication, 36
    behaviors that decrease, 42
    behaviors that increase, 41-42
    elements of, 40

Interpersonal intelligence, 73
Intrapersonal intelligence, 73
Iowa Peace Institute, 139

Jones, B. F., 57
"Just Say No" Clubs, 134-135

Kadel, S., 19, 20, 21
Kaeser, S., 44
Kempe National Center for the
    Prevention and Treatment of
    Child Abuse and Neglect, 135
Kline, M., 21, 22
Kohl, H. R., 41
Kozol, J., 24
Kreidler, W. J., 25, 27

Ladd, G. W., 90
Lasley, T., 44
Leake, D., 6
Levin, D. E., 44, 77
Levy, J., 48
Lichtenstein, R., 21, 22
Linguistic intelligence, 73
Lipka, R. P., 56
Logical-mathematical intelligence, 73
Lost generation, 1
Love, A., 40
Lytle, S. L., 69

Male Health Alliance for Life
    Extension, 139
Marzano, R. J., 57
McCarthy, C., 55
McClellan, M., 102
McConaghy, T., 7
Mendler, A. N., 29
Messing, J. K., 79
Metal detectors in schools, 3
Metropolitan Life Survey of the
    American Teacher, 2, 3
Moore, K. D., 69
Multicultural curricular approaches:
    and increasing multicultural
        peace, 62
    exceptional/culturally different
        approach, 62
    human relations approach, 62
    multicultural approach, 62

multicultural/social
    reconstructionist approach, 63
single-group studies approach, 62
Multicultural curriculum content:
    areas of use, 63-64
    content integration and, 64
    empowerment and, 63
    equity pedagogy and, 63
    flexibility of, 63
    knowledge construction and, 64
    prejudice reduction and, 63
    purposes for schoolwide use of,
        64
Multicultural education/teaching,
    60-62
    combating real problems with, 63
    nurturing multicultural peace, 61
    promoting diversity, 61
    self-directed analysis of, 61
Multicultural peace, 60-62
    definition of, 62
    nurturing, 61
Musical intelligence, 73

Narcotics Education, Inc., 135
National Association for Mediation
    in Education (NAME), 139
National Association of School
    Safety and Law Enforcement
    Officers, 109
National Center for Injury
    Prevention and Control, 105
National Coalition Building
    Institute International, 139
National Committee for
    Prevention of Child Abuse, 135
National Conference on
    Peacemaking and Conflict
    Resolution, 139
National Council on Crime and
    Delinquency, 139
National Crime Prevention
    Council, 135
National Crime Survey, 135
National Criminal Justice Refer-
    ence Service, 135-136
National Education Service, 139
National Institute Against
    Prejudice and Violence, 139

National Institute for Dispute
  Resolution, 139
National Institute of Mental
  Health, 136
National Mental Health Association, 136
National Research Council, 3
National School Safety Center, 139
National Urban League, 136
National Youth Gang Project, 136
Negotiation, definition of, 79
Negotiation skills, learning, 80
Nicholson, G., 30
Nieto, S., 63
Nonviolence, commitment of
  schools to, xvi
Novak, J., 8

Office of Juvenile Justice and
  Delinquency Prevention,
  105, 136
Office of Minority Health Resource
  Center, 137
Ordovensky, P., 109
Osborne, S., 86

Paley, V. G., 37
Parents as role models for peace,
  95, 115
Parents' Resource Institute for
  Drug Education, Inc.
  (PRIDE), 137
Parent-teacher conferences:
  hostile, 93
  ineffective, 93, 94
  informative, 93, 94
  suggestions for successful,
    94-95
Parent workshops, 87-88
  suggested topics for, 87
Parke, R. D., 90
Peace:
  communication and, 8
  curriculum and, 8
  defining, 7-8
  definition of, x
  family-school-community
    partnerships and, 8
  in classroom environment, 8,
    16-30

instruction and, 8
101 Ways to Promote, 49-51
parent involvement and, 8
resource organizations for
  teaching, 138-140
school commitment to
  nonviolence and, xvi-12
setting priorities for, 6-7
See also Multicultural peace;
  Social peace
Peaceable classrooms:
  communication in, 25
  conflict resolution in, 26
  cooperation in, 25
  culture and, 30
  description of, 25
  economic loss and, 30
  peacemaking skills/behaviors
    taught in, 25-26
  positive emotional expression
    in, 25
  space in, 26
  teachers' roles in, 27
  tolerance in, 25
Peaceable schools:
  collective involvement and, 9
  elementary/middle school
    programs for, 125-129
  middle/high school programs
    for, 129-131
  phases of planning, 9, 12
  principles for, xvi, 8, 16, 34, 55,
    68, 82, 101
  shared decision making and, 9
  See also Educational policy
    change for peaceable schools
Peace-building efforts:
  and incentives for school
    personnel, 11-12
Peace Education Foundation, Inc., 139
Peace Education Now, 139
Peaceful language:
  "no put-downs" rule, 46
  phrases to use, 46
  sexual harassment policies and, 46
  students modeling teachers, 46
  using individual's name, 47
Peace Grows, Inc., 139
Peacemaking behaviors, 58

Peacemaking skills, 105
    learning, ix
Pelfrey, W. V., 106
Peterson, K. D., 10
Phi Delta Kappa Commission on
    Discipline, 44
Physical communication, 36
    aspects of, 39-40
    teacher nonverbal cues as, 40
Physical violence, 3, 23
    forms of, 4
Pinnell, G., 44
Presseisen, B. Z., 57
Principal:
    as model of peaceful behavior, 18
    as motivational leader, 18
    leadership of, 18-19
    security personnel and, 19
    visibility of, 18
Problem solving as peacemaking
    behavior, 58
Problem-solving skills, social, 78-80
Project SHARE, 137
Project SMART, School Mediator's
    Alternative Resolution Team,
    139
Purkey, W. W., 8

Quest International, 139

Rankin, S. C., 57
Rapp, J. A., 30
Resolving Conflict Creatively
    Program (RCCP), 140
Revolutionary violence, 3
    forms of, 4
Rich, J. M., 89
Richardson, R. C., 90
Roderick, J., 40
Rodriguez, R., 48
Rose, L. C., 91
Roth, R. A., 12
Runkel, P. J., 41, 43

Safe schools:
    appearance of, 23-25
    classroom environment and, 25-27
    classroom management/
        discipline and, 28-29

creating, 19-22
effective schools research and,
    22-23
goals and, 18
inventory for, 20
principal's leadership and, 18-19
rules and procedures and, 18
staff-student relationships and, 18
Sailes, J., 2
San Diego City Schools, 17, 19
Sarason, S. B., 5
Schmuck, R. A., 41, 43
Schonfeld, D. J., 21, 22
School:
    and family, 85-86
    as community center, 102
    as major character-developing
        agent, vii
    as major socializing agent, vii
    commitment of to nonviolence, xvi
    longterm influence of on
        children's development,
        vii-viii
School, B., 38
School-based social services, 103
School Initiatives Program,
        Community Board Center
        for Policy and Training, 140
School Mediation Associates, 140
School-parent activities, 97
School personnel, communication
        among, 43-44
Schools, parent-friendly support
        for, 91-92
School security strategies:
    employee background checks, 21
    organization of crisis
        intervention team, 21-22
    providing students with personal
        safety information, 20
    providing teachers with personal
        safety information, 20
    See also Crisis management
        plans
School security systems:
    faculty involvement in creation
        of, 19
    funded, 19
    gangs and, 20-21

nonfunded, 19
parent involvement in creation
    of, 19
peace officers as, 19
posting signs as, 19
staff involvement in creation of, 19
School violence reduction, 3-4
    as America's education agenda, ix
Schubert, W. H., 56
Security coverage in schools, 3
Serious Habitual Offender
    Comprehensive Action
    Program, 106
Sleeter, C. E., 62
Socializing environments, vii
Social peace, 64-65
    cultivation of, 64
    social curriculum and, 64-65
Social problem-solving skills,
    learning, ix
Social responsibility as peacemak-
    ing behavior, 58
Southern Poverty Law Center, 140
Spatial intelligence, 73
Squires, D., 22
Stevenson, C., 71
Stevenson, D. L., 85
Stomfay-Stitz, A. M., 7
Students, adult supervision of, 88-89
    lack of and school problems, 88
Students, understanding:
    in high school, 76
    in middle school, 75-76
    in primary grades, 74
    in upper elementary grades,
        74-75
Suhor, C., 57
Surveillance/warning devices in
    schools, 3
Sweeney, J. T., 22

TARGET, 137
Teaching styles:
    authoritarian, 69
    democratic, 69-70
    laissez-faire, 69, 70
Tennessee Education Association
    and Appalachia Educational
    Laboratory, 3

Thomason, J., 71
Thomson, B. J., 46
Tolerance as peacemaking behav-
    ior, 58
Tomlinson, L. M., 92
Toughlove, 137

U.S. Department of Education, 18,
    24, 27, 29, 84
U.S. Department of Justice,
    Community Relations
    Service, 140
Useem, E. L., 85

Values:
    family versus school, 89-90
    instilling at home, 90-91
    instilling in school, 90-91
Verbal violence, 3, 23
    forms of, 4
Violence:
    consequences of witnessing, 102
    definition of, 3
    types of, 3-4
    See also specific types of violence
Violence prevention programs:
    community members'
        involvement in, 4
    cultural diversity awareness
        and, 4
    decision makers in, 7
    early childhood interventions, 4
    implementing, 2
    limited access to firearms and, 5
    mass media and, 5
    police/community leaders and, 5
    prejudice/hostility educational
        programs, 5
    psychological health services
        and, 5
    school-based interventions, 4
    youth alcohol/drug use
        reduction and, 5

Walkie-talkies in schools, 3
Wayson, W., 44
Weapons, use of in schools, 3